Kenneth E. Hagin

Second Edition
Eighth Printing 1997

ISBN 0-89276-043-5

In the U.S. write:
Kenneth Hagin Ministries
P.O. Box 50126
Tulsa, OK 74150-0126

In Canada write:
Kenneth Hagin Ministries
Box 335, Station D,
Etobicoke, Ontario, M9A 4X3

Cover photo by Bill Alderman

OTHER BOOKS BY KENNETH E. HAGIN
(A partial listing)

Preface

Feed your faith daily! It is of utmost importance to your walk with the Lord. I've written these bite-size pieces of "faith food" to aid you in making sure your faith is fed daily.

F. F. Bosworth said, "Most Christians feed their bodies three hot meals a day, their spirits one cold snack a week, and then they wonder why they are so weak in faith."

Say the confessions found on the bottom of each page aloud. Close your eyes and repeat them. They are based on God's Word. When you hear yourself say these confessions, they will register on your spirit. And when God's Word gets down into your spirit, it will control your life!

Kenneth E. Hagin

About the Author

The ministry of Kenneth E. Hagin has spanned more than 50 years since God miraculously healed him of a deformed heart and incurable blood disease at the age of 17. Today the scope of Kenneth Hagin Ministries is worldwide. The ministry's radio program, "Faith Seminar of the Air," is heard coast-to-coast in the U.S., and reaches more than 80 nations. Other outreaches include: *The Word of Faith,* a free monthly magazine; All Faiths' Crusades, conducted nationwide; RHEMA Correspondence Bible School; RHEMA Bible Training Center; RHEMA Alumni Association and RHEMA Ministerial Association International; and a prison ministry outreach.

God Is a Spirit

But the hour cometh, and now is, when the true worshippers shall worship the Father in spirit and in truth: for the Father seeketh such to worship him. God is a Spirit: and they that worship him must worship him in spirit and in truth. — JOHN 4:23,24

God is a Spirit.

Spiritual things are more real than *material* things. They have to be, because God, who is a Spirit, created all material things.

God's Unseen Ability brought into being everything we know upon the earth in the natural realm by simply saying, "Let there be. . . ."

You cannot know God, or touch God, or become acquainted with God *physically*.

You cannot know God, or touch God, or communicate with God *mentally*.

God is a Spirit. And, thank God, you can reach Him with *your* spirit. Your human spirit can come to know God. Your spirit can become acquainted with God. Your spirit can communicate with God. Your spirit can worship God!

Confession: *The hour now is when the true worshippers worship the Father in spirit and in truth. I am a true worshipper. God is a Spirit. I worship God in spirit and in truth. My spirit knows God. My spirit becomes better and better acquainted with God every day. My spirit communicates with God. My spirit worships God.*

In His Image

And God said, Let us make man in our image, after our likeness. . . . So God created man in his own image, in the image of God created he him. . . .

— GENESIS 1:26,27

For the Lord taketh pleasure in his people. . . .

— PSALM 149:4

If man is made in the likeness of God, and God is a Spirit, then man, of necessity, must be a spirit.

God made man for His own pleasure. He made man to fellowship with Him. Man is not an animal. Man is in the same class with God; otherwise, he couldn't fellowship with God.

Did you ever try to fellowship with a cow? Cows are in a different kingdom than you are in. They are in a different class. You can't fellowship with them.

But we can fellowship with one another. And we can fellowship with God. Because we are in the same class of being as God.

God is a Spirit. And man, created in the image and likeness of God, is also a spirit being.

Confession: *God is a Spirit. And I am a spirit. I am created in God's image and in His likeness. I am in the same class of being as God. I can give God pleasure. I can fellowship with Him.*

Man of the Heart

Whose adorning let it not be that outward adorning of plaiting the hair, and of wearing of gold, or of putting on of apparel; But let it be the HIDDEN MAN OF THE HEART, in that which is not corruptible, even the ornament of a meek and quiet SPIRIT, which is in the sight of God of great price. — 1 PETER 3:3,4

No one knows what you look like! They may think they do, but they don't. You — the real you — are a hidden man. You are a spirit; you have a soul; and you live in a body (1 Thess. 5:23). What people see is only the "house" you live in.

I've heard ministers quote two-thirds of First Peter 3:3 and say that women shouldn't fix their hair and shouldn't wear gold. But if that's what Peter meant, then women shouldn't wear clothes, either! Because if Peter told women not to plait their hair, and not to wear gold, then he also told them not to put on apparel. (Apparel is clothing.)

No, Peter is really saying — probably because women are more prone to do this — "Don't spend all your time on your hair, on your clothes, and on the *outward* man. See to it first of all that *the hidden man of the heart* — that's the spiritual man, the real man, the inward man — is adorned with a meek and a quiet *spirit.*"

Confession: *I am a spirit. I am a child of the Father of spirits. I have a soul. And I live in a body. I see to the adorning of the real me — the hidden man of the heart.*

The Inward Man

For which cause we faint not; but though our outward man perish, yet the inward man is renewed day by day.

— 2 CORINTHIANS 4:16

The outward man, or the body, is decaying. It's growing older, just as the house you may live in at 504 Chestnut Street is growing older.

But do you know what? *You* are not getting any older!

What does the Scripture say about the real you? Does it say, "Yet the inward man is perishing?" No. "Is decaying?" No. "Is growing older?" No! It says, " ... *the inward man is RENEWED DAY BY DAY*"!

You will never be any older than you are right now!

You're no older now than you were a few years ago. You may know more, but you're not any older.

The inward man — the real you — is renewed day by day!

Confession: *I am a spirit being. I am the child of the Father of spirits. The real me is a "hidden man," an inward man. I am not getting any older. I am being renewed day by day. I am an eternal spirit being.*

4

Eternal Unseen Things

While we look not at the things which are seen, but at the things which are not seen: for the things which are seen are temporal; but the things which are not seen are eternal.... For we know that if our earthly house of this tabernacle were dissolved, we have a building of God, an house not made with hands, eternal in the heavens.

— 2 CORINTHIANS 4:18; 5:1

The outward man is seen.

The inward man is that "hidden man." He is unseen. Paul is still talking about this inward man we read about from yesterday's Scripture text, Second Corinthians 4:16. Paul is saying that this inward man is unseen — and he is eternal.

Our "earthly house of this tabernacle" is the outward man Paul was talking about in the sixteenth verse. Our earthly house (body) is decaying. When it dies, is put into the grave, is dissolved, and goes back to dust — *that is not the end!*

The inward man is eternal!

The hidden man of the heart is eternal!

The hidden man is a spirit man — and he is eternal!

You are a spirit — and you are eternal!

Confession: *I am an eternal spirit. I look not to the things which are seen. I look at the things which are not seen. For the things which are seen are temporal, but the things which are not seen are eternal!*

Confident, Knowing

Therefore we are always confident, knowing that, whilst we are at home in the body, we are absent from the Lord: (For we walk by faith, not by sight:) We are confident, I say, and willing rather to be absent from the body, and to be present with the Lord.

—2 CORINTHIANS 5:6-8

". . . confident, knowing. . . ." I like that! Not hoping. Not guessing. Not maybe so. But knowing! Knowing that while "we" are at home in the body, "we" are absent from the Lord. Yes, His Spirit is in our hearts, crying, "Abba, Father," but Jesus Christ, with a physical, flesh-and-bone resurrected body is at the right hand of the Father in heaven. And when "we" are absent from the body, "we" will be present with Him there.

Who is "we"?

At the time of his physical death, man leaves his body. When he does, he is no less man than when he had his body. I don't have space here to recount my entire testimony concerning my experience of dying (for the complete account, please see my minibook entitled, *I Went to Hell*). But I do want to say this: When I was *outside* my body, I was no less man than I was when I was *inside* my body. To me, I was just as real as I am now. I had the same shape. I had the same form. I had the same size. I knew everything I knew before I left my body.

Confession: *The real me lives inside my body. The real me is an eternal spirit being that will never die!*

6

Gain!

For to me to live is Christ, and to die is gain.
— PHILIPPIANS 1:21

When the body dies, the inward man still lives. In today's text, Paul was talking about physical death — and he said it is *gain.*

That does away with the theory that when a man is dead, he's dead like a dog, and that's the end of it. There certainly wouldn't be any gain to that.

It also does away with the theory that when you die, you just float around like a cloud in the sky. There wouldn't be any gain to that, either.

And it does away with the theory of reincarnation — and that's all it is — a theory. It's certainly not scriptural. Some people think they will be born again into this life — that the next time they might be a cow, or a horse, or even a fly. There wouldn't be any *gain* to coming back as a cow — you might get eaten. If you were a mosquito, you might get squashed. How foolish people can become when they leave the Bible and get off into false teachings!

The truth is just as the Bible presents it: At physical death, the born-again believer — an eternal spirit being — departs to be with Christ, and that is gain!

Confession: *For "me" to live in this physical body is Christ. The life of Christ dwells within the real me — the man on the inside, the eternal spirit being.*

Our Choice

For to me to live is Christ, and to die is gain. But if I live in the flesh, this is the fruit of my labour: yet what I shall choose I wot not. For I am in a strait betwixt two, having a desire to depart, and to be with Christ; which is far better: Nevertheless to abide in the flesh is more needful for you. And having this confidence, I know that I shall abide and continue with you all for your furtherance and joy of faith.
— **PHILIPPIANS 1:21-25**

Paul is talking here about physical death. Of course, the *real* Paul, the inner man, is not going to die. He's going to go on living either way: departing and being with Christ, *or* abiding in the flesh.

Paul said he hadn't *decided* yet. "I'm in a strait," he said, "between the two. I want to go on and be with Christ, which is far better." (If Paul had just said it would be better, that would have been wonderful, but he said it's even better than better!) Then he said, "Yet I know to abide in the flesh is more needful for you." If Paul was present in the flesh, he could teach and minister to these people. That was more needful for them.

Notice that *Paul* is making the choice. He didn't say, "I'm going to leave it up to God, and whatever God chooses, I will accept." Since God has given you a choice in the matter, that kind of philosophy is really letting the devil dominate you. We have more to do with deciding to live or die than we have thought!

Confession: *The real me is an eternal spirit.*

Three Dimensions of Man

And the very God of peace sanctify you wholly; and I pray God your whole spirit and soul and body be preserved blameless unto the coming of our Lord Jesus Christ.

— 1 THESSALONIANS 5:23

It will help your spiritual growth immeasurably to know the difference between your *spirit* and your *soul.*

Many people believe that "spirit" and "soul" are the same thing. Even preachers believe this! They preach about the soul as if it were the spirit.

But they can't be the same thing. It would be just as scriptural to say that the body and the soul are the same, as it would be to say that the spirit and the soul are the same. But Hebrews 4:12 says that by the Word of God, soul and spirit can be divided.

To help you understand the three dimensions of man, go through this process of elimination:

(1) With my *body* I contact the *physical* realm.

(2) With my *spirit* I contact the *spiritual* realm.

(3) With my *soul* I contact the *intellectual* and *emotional* realms.

Man is a spirit. The *spirit* is the part of man that knows God. Man possesses a *soul* — the intellect, the sensibilities, the will. And man lives in a *body.*

Confession: *I am a son of God. I am a child of God. With my spirit I contact my Father in the spiritual realm.*

9

Heart Hunger

And Jesus said unto them, I am the bread of life: he that cometh to me shall never hunger; and he that believeth on me shall never thirst.
— JOHN 6:35

Before Adam sinned, he walked and talked with God. Adam had fellowship with God.

But when Adam fell, his spirit became estranged, or separated, from God.

Since that day, in the life of every person born into this world, there is a heart hunger; a spirit hunger.

This heart hunger causes men to seek something to satisfy it. Some look to worldly possessions. Some look to false religions of this world. Yet nothing can satisfy this heart hunger but God.

Although this heart hunger may have driven a man to all kinds of things, it ends when he finds Jesus Christ. When he becomes acquainted with the Lord Jesus Christ and receives eternal life and is born again, he becomes the child of God. Man then has a relationship with God! He can fellowship with God! His heart hunger is satisfied!

Confession: *I came to Jesus. Therefore, I shall never hunger. I believe on Jesus. Therefore, I shall never thirst. I am related to God. He is my Father. I have fellowship with Him. My heart is satisfied!*

Gift of God

For the wages of sin is death; but the gift of God is eternal life through Jesus Christ our Lord.

— ROMANS 6:23

God contacts men through their *spirits.*

When the Word of God is preached to a sinner who has never heard the Gospel, and conviction comes upon him, it's not a physical feeling — it's not a mental something (he may not even understand it) — but it's down deep on the inside. The Spirit of God through the Word of God is contacting the spirit of that sinner!

Then, when he responds to the call of God and the Gospel message, his spirit is born again. His spirit is recreated by receiving *eternal life.*

Receiving eternal life is the most miraculous event in life. It's called the New Birth. It's called the new creation. It is, in reality, God imparting His very nature, substance, and being to our human spirits.

It is described in Second Corinthians 5:17,18.

The New Birth is God actually giving birth to a man. And this instantaneous New Birth takes place not in the body, not in the soul, but in the spirit of man! The spirit of man becomes a brand-new, miracle creation in God!

Confession: *I am a brand-new, miracle creation in Christ. God gave me the gift of eternal life. He imparted to my spirit His very nature, substance, and being. Residing in my own spirit is everything I'll ever need to put me over in life.*

11

Saving Your Soul

Of his own will begat he us with the word of truth, that we should be a kind of firstfruits of his creatures.... Wherefore lay apart all filthiness and superfluity of naughtiness, and receive with meekness the engrafted word, which is able to save your souls.

— JAMES 1:18,21

What about our *souls?* Aren't our souls saved when we're born again? No. There are many Christians who have been saved and filled with the Holy Spirit for years whose souls are not saved yet!

Some have lived and died without their souls being saved. Did they go to heaven? Certainly. They were children of God, and their spirits were born of God.

The soul, you see, is not born again. The saving of the soul is a *process.*

The Epistle of James was written not to sinners, but to Christians. And James was telling us that our souls are not saved yet. James 1:21 used to bother me, until I found out the difference between the spirit and the soul.

A man's *spirit* — the innermost man — receives eternal life and is born again. But his intellect and his emotions — which constitute his *soul* — still have to be dealt with. They must be renewed.

Confession: *I am a spirit. I have a soul. I live in a body. "I" am begotten of God by the Word of truth. "I" am born again. Now I receive with meekness the engrafted Word which contains the power to save the soul which I possess. My intellect is being renewed with the Word of God.*

Restoring the Soul

He restoreth my soul....   — PSALM 23:3

I beseech you therefore, brethren, by the mercies of God, that ye present your bodies a living sacrifice, holy, acceptable unto God, which is your reasonable service. And be not conformed to this world: but be ye transformed by the renewing of your mind, that ye may prove what is that good, and acceptable, and perfect, will of God.

        — ROMANS 12:1,2

Paul, writing to born-again, Spirit-filled Christians in Romans 12, tells them to do something with their bodies and their minds. Man's spirit is born again at the New Birth — but he still has the same old body and the same soul. He is to present his *body* to God, and he is to see to it that his *mind* is renewed.

The Hebrew word translated "restoreth" in Psalm 23 and the Greek word translated "renewed" in Romans 12:2 have just about the same meaning. For example, a valuable antique chair which looks like a wreck can be *restored.* Afterwards it's still the same chair, but it has been *renewed.* A man's *spirit* is never restored; it's *born again,* or *recreated.* But his *soul* is *restored* when his mind becomes renewed with the Word of God.

The greatest need of the Church today is for believers to have their minds renewed with the Word of God. It is the Word of God that restores souls, renews souls, and saves souls!

Confession: *I see to it daily that my mind is renewed with the Word of God. Therefore, I am not conformed to this world. My mind is renewed to think like God thinks.*

Why Did Jesus Come?

*. . . I am come that they might have life, and that they might
have it more abundantly.*   — JOHN 10:10

Why did Jesus come?

Did Jesus come to give us some creed to live
by? Did He come to give us a code of ethics — a
list of "do's and don'ts" — to straighten us out?
Did He come to start a new religion, or to found
a new church?

No! Jesus came for one purpose: That we might
have *life,* and that we might have it *more abundantly!*

This word "life" is the biggest word of the
Gospel. Man needed life, because he was spiritually
dead. Spiritual death, which is the nature of the
devil, was imparted to man at the fall of man, when
Adam sinned. The eradication of this devil-nature
is what God has worked toward in all the ages. It
was the reason why Jesus came to the earth. Jesus
stated, ". . . *I am come that ye might have life. . . .*"

The only thing that will meet man's need is the
nature of God: eternal life. Nothing can take its
place.

When a person receives eternal life, he receives
the nature of God, the life of God, into himself.
This is that divine act that changes a man from
the family of Satan to the family of God instantly.

Confession: *The life of God has been imparted to my spirit.
I am alive unto God. The life of God — the nature of God
— is imparted to my spirit. I will let the life and nature
of God that's in me, dominate me.*

Divine Nature

Whereby are given unto us exceeding great and precious promises: that by these ye might be partakers of the divine nature, having escaped the corruption that is in the world through lust.

— 2 PETER 1:4

When you became a child of God, God imparted His own nature — eternal life — to you. This life, this nature, this being, this substance of God, instantly changed your spirit.

You passed out of spiritual death — the realm of Satan — into life, which is the realm of God (1 John 3:14). You passed out of the dominion of Satan into the dominion of Christ.

When you received eternal life, the satanic nature passed out of you. The corruption from which you have escaped (2 Peter 1:4) is spiritual death, the satanic nature.

The satanic nature passed out of you, not theoretically, but actually. Second Corinthians 5:17 states, ". . . old things are passed away. . . ." And God's nature came into you.

Now you are a partaker of God's divine nature — the nature of God — the life of God!

Confession: *God's life is in me. God's nature is in me. God's ability is in me. God's wisdom is in me. For me to fail, God would have to fail. And God can never fail! I am a partaker of His divine nature.*

15

Zoe

For as the Father hath life [zoe] in himself; so hath he given to the Son to have life [zoe] in himself.

— JOHN 5:26

The Greek word translated "life" in our text today is *zoe.* It is pronounced zō-ā.

Reading through the *King James Version,* or any English translation, when you see the word "life," you might think it's always talking about the same thing, but it isn't. Three other Greek words in the New Testament are translated as "life." Briefly, these words and their meanings are: *psuche,* natural life, or human life; *bios,* manner of life; and *anastrophe,* behavior.

Zoe means eternal life, or God's life. It is God's nature. It is life as God has it — that which the Father has in Himself — and that which the Incarnate Son has in Himself. It is called *eternal life, everlasting life,* and sometimes just *life* in the Word of God.

No matter what "manner of life" or "behavior" you have, it won't do you any good unless you have *zoe!* And that's what Jesus came to bring you!

Confession: *For as the Father hath zoe in Himself, so hath He given to the Son to have zoe in Himself. Jesus said, "I am come that you might have zoe, and that you might have it more abundantly." I have zoe in myself. And I have it more abundantly!*

Helping Others to Life

And many other signs truly did Jesus in the presence of his disciples, which are not written in this book: But these are written, that ye might believe that Jesus is the Christ, the Son of God; and that believing ye might have life [zoe] through his name. — JOHN 20:30,31

Jesus did many things that are not recorded in John's Gospel, or in the other Gospels. But the things that are recorded in the Gospels are recorded for a purpose. What is this purpose? ". . . that ye might believe that Jesus is the Christ, the Son of God; and that believing ye might have zoe *through his name.*"

The object is that we might receive eternal life!

You as a Christian need to know how to help others receive eternal life. The first step is to get them to read or hear what is written in the Gospels so they may know that Jesus is the Christ, the Son of God, and that as the Son of God, He has made spiritual life available to spiritually dead men.

John 3:15,16 shows us how: *"That whosoever believeth in him* [Jesus] *should not perish, but have eternal life* [zoe]. *For God so loved the world, that he gave his only begotten Son, that whosoever believeth in him should not perish, but have everlasting life* [zoe]."

Confession: *I believe that Jesus is the Christ, the Son of God. And, believing, I received zoe through His Name. I shall never perish. I have zoe. I have the life of God — I have the nature of God — abiding in me.*

17

What To Believe

For I delivered unto you first of all that which I also received, how that Christ died for our sins according to the scriptures; And that he was buried, and that he rose again the third day according to the scriptures.

— 1 CORINTHIANS 15:3,4

I read some time ago about a so-called minister of the Gospel. He was a man of some acclaim, and reporters interviewed him when he arrived in a large city about an article he had written. In the article, he had stated, "There is some question as to whether Jesus ever rose from the dead. And it doesn't really make any difference whether He did or not."

It makes all the difference in the world!

It makes the difference between heaven and hell! It makes the difference between being lost or being saved!

It makes the difference between spiritual life and spiritual death — because that's the way you receive eternal life. That's the way you are born again — by believing that Jesus Christ is the Son of God, that He died for your sins according to the Scriptures, and that He arose from the dead!

Confession: *I believe that Jesus Christ is the Son of God. I believe that He died for my sins according to the Scriptures. I believe that He was raised from the dead for my justification; that is, that I might be set right with God. I believe in my heart that I am the righteousness of God. I am made right with God through what Jesus did.*

Receive Him

But as many as received him [Jesus Christ], *to them gave he power* [the right] *to become the sons of God, even to them that believe on his name.* — JOHN 1:12

Receiving Jesus Christ is an act of the will. So man acts on the Word of God by an act of his will. Man knows he is without a Savior, without an approach to God, without eternal life, so he can look up to God and pray, in essence:

Father, I come to You in the Name of the Lord Jesus Christ. I know You will not turn me away, or cast me out, because You said in your Word, ". . . him that cometh to me I will in no wise cast out." I believe in my heart that Jesus Christ is the Son of God. I believe that He died for my sins, according to the Scriptures. I believe that He was raised from the dead for my justification, according to the Scriptures. "Justification" means that I might be set right with God. I believe that because of His death, burial, and resurrection, I am set right with God. So I receive Jesus as my Savior, and I confess Him as my Lord. Your Word says, "Whosoever shall call upon the name of the Lord shall be saved." I am calling on You now, so I know I am saved. And You said, "If thou shalt confess with thy mouth the Lord Jesus, and shalt believe in thine heart that God hath raised him from the dead, thou shalt be saved." I'm confessing that with my mouth. I believe it in my heart. So I am saved. You said, ". . . with the heart man believeth unto righteousness." And with my heart I believe that I am made right with God. And You said, ". . . with the mouth confession is made unto salvation." So with my mouth I confess, I am saved! Thank You, Lord!

Hath

Verily, verily, I say unto you, He that heareth my word, and believeth on him that sent me, HATH everlasting life [zoe], and shall not come into condemnation; but is passed from death unto life.
— JOHN 5:24

Hath! You've got eternal life *now!* You're not going to get it when you get to heaven; you've got *zoe* now!

But if you don't know about the life — if you don't know what it is, or how to walk in the light of it — you'll never be able to enjoy the realities of it.

You can have something in the natural and not know you have it, and it won't do you any good. For example, sometime before Christmas of 1947, I decided to put away a little money for my wife's gift. I started by putting a $20 bill in the secret compartment of my billfold. Then I forgot all about it. A few weeks later, I ran out of gas. I didn't have any money to buy any gas, so I had to call one of the deacons of the church to come and get me. Sometime later I was going through the billfold and found that $20. Now, you couldn't really say I didn't have the money when I ran out of gas. I had it, but I didn't know it, so it didn't do me any good.

God gave us His Word so we can find out what we have — eternal life — and then walk in the light of it.

Confession: *I will learn to walk in the light of what I have — eternal life.*

Change

*For in Christ Jesus neither circumcision availeth any thing,
nor uncircumcision, but a new creature.*

— GALATIANS 6:15

*For neither is circumcision [now] of any importance, nor
uncircumcision, but [only] a new creation [the result of a
new birth and a new nature in Christ Jesus, the Messiah].*

— GALATIANS 6:15 *Amplified*

The first thing *zoe* does in a man is to change
his nature. It changes his spirit. *Zoe* makes him
a new creature. All things become new in his
inward man, or spirit.

What this new man, or new creature, must do
now is allow his inward man to dominate him.
When we believers allow our spirits to dominate
us, we permit the life of God in us to dominate us.

People are able to see the effects of this life of
God within us. They see changes in a person's
habits, conduct, speech, and so forth. Criminals
become law-abiding citizens. Thieves become
honest. Drunkards become sober. Prostitutes
become moral. No case is incurable!

With this life (*zoe*) that comes into man, there
comes a new kind of love (*agape*). And when the
believer allows it to dominate him, it will destroy
the cause of friction in homes: It will eliminate
selfishness.

Confession: *I am a new creature. The life and nature of
God has been imparted to my spirit. God is love. I will let
His life dominate me. I will let His love dominate me.*

Development

In him [Jesus] *was life* [zoe]; *and the life* [zoe] *was the light of men.* — JOHN 1:4

The life that came into you at the New Birth can affect your mental processes by governing your thinking and your intellect.

It certainly did mine. I received eternal life as a teenaged boy on the bed of sickness, April 22, 1933. Then on August 8, 1934, I was healed by the power of God through faith and prayer.

After my healing, I returned to high school. During the sixteen months I had been bedfast, I had missed one school year. And in the two years of high school I'd completed before, I had been a "D" student.

At that time, I didn't have a Greek concordance, so I didn't know about *zoe*. But I had my Bible, and the Spirit of God led me. Every day as I went to school I would say this:

"In Him was life, and the life was the light of men. That life is in me. The life of God is in me. That life is the light. (I knew light stood for development.) That life is developing me. That life is developing my spirit. That life is developing my mentality. I've got God in me. I've got God's wisdom in me. I've got God's life in me. I've got God's power in me."

Confession: *Make your own confession today based on John 1:4, and confess the life of God within you as your light.*

Heart Purpose

But Daniel purposed in his heart that he would not defile himself with the portion of the king's meat, nor with the wine which he drank: therefore he requested of the prince of the eunuchs that he might not defile himself.

— DANIEL 1:8

I had two favorite Scriptures I either read or quoted to the Lord and on which I based my confession every morning as I walked to high school. The first was John 1:4. The second was the first chapter of Daniel.

Read Daniel chapter one and see how Daniel and the three Hebrew children, although they were captives, were chosen as students in the king's college.

The Bible says that Daniel "purposed in his heart." I used this phrase with the Lord. I knew that even though I wasn't living under the Old Covenant, there still was a principle here I could abide by.

You see, the Jews weren't supposed to eat certain meats, but that's not so with us. The Word of God says under the New Covenant, "... *every creature of God is good, and nothing to be refused, if it be received with thanksgiving: For it is sanctified by the word of God and prayer*" (1 Tim. 4:4,5).

So I acted upon the same principle Daniel did. I said this to the Lord every morning: "I purpose in my heart to walk in the light of life."

Confession: *I purpose in my heart to walk in the light of life. I purpose to walk in the light of the life of God in me.*

Favor

*Now God had brought Daniel into favour and tender love
with the prince of the eunuchs.* — DANIEL 1:9

I didn't know anything about confession of
faith when I was first saved as a teenager. But
somehow my spirit impelled me to say these
things. Second Corinthians 5:17 was a favorite
Scripture of mine. I would tell everybody I met,
"I'm a new creature!" They'd reply, "What's
that?" And I would start preaching on it. Before
I knew it, I'd have a crowd gathered around me
right there on the street!

Every morning, as I walked to school, I made
my confessions based on John 1:4 and Daniel
chapter one. Sometimes a bunch of us students
took up the whole street as we walked along.
Sometimes they thought I was crazy, but I'd
explain it to them as we walked along.

I would say, "Now, you see, Daniel had favor
with the prince of eunuchs (or, as we would call
him in modern times, the dean of the college). And
it was God who gave Daniel favor with him."

Then I would say to God, "God, give me favor
with every teacher. Thank You for it. It is mine."

Confession: *God, give me favor with* [your teacher, your
mate, your business associate, etc.]. *Thank You for it.
Favor is mine.*

Knowledge and Skill

As for these four children, God gave them knowledge and skill in all learning and wisdom: and Daniel had understanding in all visions and dreams.

— DANIEL 1:17

"... *God gave them*...."

God gave Daniel and the other three Hebrew children, knowledge and all skill.

Eternal life is the nature of God. You've got God's nature in you. Know that! Believe that! Confess that! Then that nature will begin to dominate you!

Learn to walk in the light of life. Learn to put that life into practice in your being. Walking in the light of that life will enhance your entire personality, and will increase your intelligence.

Confession: *I am a new creation. I am born again. I am a new creature. I have the life and nature of God in my spirit. That life is the light of men. I purpose to walk in the light of life. God's life is in me. God's knowledge is in me. God's skill is in me. God's ability is in me. God's wisdom is in me. He is instructing me. He is leading me. I am a child of God. The Spirit of God in me is leading me. I'll follow His leading. I'll walk in the light of life.*

Ten Times Better

Now at the end of the days that the king had said he should bring them in [three years later] ... *the king communed with them; and among them all was found NONE like Daniel, Hananiah, Mishael, and Azariah: therefore stood they before the king. And in ALL matters of wisdom and understanding, that the king inquired of them, he found them TEN TIMES BETTER than all the magicians and astrologers that were in all his realm.*

— DANIEL 1:18-20

Each day I said, "God, give me favor with every teacher. Thank You for it. It is mine. Now impart to me — because I have the life and nature of God in me — knowledge and skill in all learning and wisdom that I may be ten times better ..."

Now, I'm not bragging on me; I'm bragging on what God gave me. Because although I had been a "D" student before my sickness, after being born again and healed, I was the only student in my classes who made a straight "A" report card.

I could take a history book — and they tested me on this — read a chapter I'd never read before, put the book down, and recite it word for word. Now, I couldn't do that because I had developed my memory. I didn't know a thing in the world about memorization. I was able to do that because I looked to my spirit.

Most believers have never developed their spirits as they could have. They have just never really walked in the light of what they've had all the time.

Confession: *I purpose to develop my spirit. I purpose to walk in the light of life.*

Miracle Life

For ye were sometimes darkness, but now are ye light in the Lord: walk as children of light.

— EPHESIANS 5:8

The greatest miracle I've seen of eternal life affecting mentality was in a girl I'll call Mary. Mary had spent seven years in the first grade without even learning to write her name. The authorities asked her parents to take her out of school when she was 14 years old.

As an 18 year old, she behaved like a 2 year old. If she happened not to be sitting with her mother in the service, she would crawl or slide under the pews, or else she would lift up her skirt and step over them, to get to where her mother was.

Then one night, during an evangelistic revival meeting, Mary came to the altar. There she received eternal life — the nature of God. A drastic change occurred instantly. The very next night she sat in the service and behaved like any 18-year-old young lady. She had fixed her hair and had dressed up. Her mentality seemed to have increased overnight.

Soon afterwards, she went away to visit relatives, and there she met and married a neighboring farm boy. Many years later, I learned that after the accidental death of her husband, she had become a prosperous businesswoman who was her own financier and contractor on a housing addition she was building in her city!

Confession: *I walk as a child of light in the Lord. I walk in the light of life.*

27

Walking in the Light of Life

Then spake Jesus again unto them, saying, I am the light of the world: he that followeth me shall not walk in darkness, but shall have the light of life. — JOHN 8:12

I began to see some truths about eternal life before our children were born. And I believed by the grace of God that I could walk in the light of eternal life. (If God tells me in His Word I can, then I can.) I knew walking in the light of eternal life would affect my children, and so I could predict how they would turn out. I also predicted how some of the babies born in our church around the same time would turn out. I could do that because I knew what sort of light their parents were walking in and how that would affect the children. I was right one hundred percent of the time.

People can have eternal life, but if they don't walk in the light of it, developing themselves — if they don't take advantage of that life and nature — things won't turn out right in their lives. We *have* eternal life, but we have to *appropriate* it. We have to walk in the light of it.

Children should have the privilege of being born into homes where eternal life and the love of God are present. I've observed how children whose parents have this life *and walk in the light of it* respond to religious training. Such children have a fineness of spirit others do not have. They are easier to discipline, and they have keener intellects. Teenagers who receive eternal life and allow that life to dominate them are more mentally efficient afterwards than they were before they were saved.

Confession: *God's life is in me. That life is the light, and it affects my development. I walk in the light of it. It affects my home!*

Made Manifest

Always bearing about in the body the dying of the Lord Jesus, that the life [zoe] *also of Jesus might be made manifest in our body. For we which live are alway delivered unto death for Jesus' sake, that the life* [zoe] *also of Jesus might be made manifest in our mortal flesh.*

— 2 CORINTHIANS 4:10,11

Paul is talking about *zoe* being manifested in our mortal bodies. But he's not talking about the resurrection of the body, for mortal means "subject to death." When we're raised up, we'll have an immortal body.

No, Paul is talking about having this *zoe* life of God which came into our spirits at the New Birth manifested during *this* life — in our death-doomed mortal flesh!

I am convinced that if we learn how to walk in the light of life, and let that life which came into us at our New Birth dominate us, there is no reason at all why we can't live to a great age, if Jesus tarries His coming. I know the outward man is decaying, but the *zoe* life of God can be made manifest in our mortal flesh!

Confession: *Thank You, Father, that the life that is in my spirit can also quicken my mortal body. It can make my body full of life, health, and healing. Because in the great plan of redemption, which You planned and sent the Lord Jesus Christ to consummate, there is not only the rebirth of my spirit, but there is also healing for my physical being. "Himself took my infirmities and bare my sicknesses." What Jesus bore, I need not bear. By Jesus' stripes I am healed. I am made whole — spiritually, physically, and mentally. According to the Word of God, I am healed! I am whole!*

Conductor of Life

... God hath given to us eternal life, and this life is in his Son. He that hath the Son hath life....

— 1 JOHN 5:11,12

Jesus said, *"Go ye into all the world, and preach the gospel to every creature. . . . And these signs shall follow them that believe . . ."* (Mark 16:15,17). One of the signs Jesus said would follow *believers* — not the Early Church, not apostles, not pastors, not preachers, but *believers* — is, *". . . they shall lay hands on the sick, and they shall recover"* (Mark 16:18).

Why? Because the life of God is in believers!

Sometimes people are specially anointed to minister healing, but that isn't what Mark 16 is talking about! Every born-again believer has the life of God, the nature of God, the God-kind of life, in him — and by the laying on of hands, that life can be imparted into the physical bodies of others!

That's why you should lay hands on the sick. When you lay hands on them, that life of God in you is conducted through your hands to others. Often, you'll be conscious of that life flowing right out of you into them. You've got the *life* of God in you! You've got the *nature* of God in you! God's a healing God. Put God's power to work! That's how God works — through your own hands. God's not here on earth in Person, but He is *in you* by His Spirit!

Confession: *I am a believing one. I have the life of God in me. And God is a healing God. I lay hands on the sick, and they recover.*

The Lordship of Jesus

Therefore we are buried with him by baptism into death: that like as Christ was raised up from the dead by the glory of the Father, even so we also should walk in newness of life.

— ROMANS 6:4

Some translations of Romans 10:9 read, ". . . if thou shalt confess with thy mouth Jesus as Lord, and shalt believe in thy heart . . . thou shalt be saved." That means you must confess Jesus as your Lord and acknowledge His lordship over your life in order to be saved.

The reason for this is obvious. We've been the servants and the subjects — as well as the children — of Satan, the enemy of God. We have belonged to the kingdom of the devil. Now we want to leave that kingdom and become "naturalized citizens" of God's kingdom. But before we can do this, we must swear allegiance to the new fatherland, so to speak. We must make an absolute, unconditional break with our old fatherland. So, the Bible says, we must confess Jesus Christ as Lord. He is the new Ruler of our intellectual life as well as our heart, or spiritual life.

Some want to have Jesus as *Savior*, but not as *Lord*. They want Him as their Savior from hell, but they don't want Him as their Lord and Ruler on earth. You can't really have one without the other.

Confession: *I walk in the newness of life. Jesus Christ is my Savior. Jesus is my Lord. Lord Jesus, I live in your kingdom now, and I acknowledge your lordship over my life. I want to have your will and your way in every area of my life.*

The Lord Christ

And whatsoever ye do, do it heartily, as to the Lord, and not unto men; Knowing that of the Lord ye shall receive the reward of the inheritance: for ye serve the Lord Christ.
— COLOSSIANS 3:23,24

When Jesus becomes your Lord, He will want to have something to say about the kind of books you read — about the amusements you enjoy — about the governing of your physical body.

If Jesus is your Lord, He will want to have something to say about your finances — how you make your money — and how you use your money.

If Jesus is your Lord, He will want to have something to say about your marriage — about your children — about your home. He will want to dictate to you regarding your vocation in life and where you live.

Yes, Jesus will want to enter every area of your life, if He's your Lord. And I want Him to be my Lord, don't you? That's what makes the Christian life blessed. The lordship of Jesus strips life of its weakness, frailty, and human guidance. It lifts life out of the realm of the natural and into the supernatural.

Confession: *Lord Jesus, I want You to have your way in every area of my life. I want You to have your say-so in every area of my life — in the books I read, in the company I keep, in the amusements I enjoy, in my companions, in my marriage, in my home, in my finances, and in the way I spend my time.*

The Living Word

For there are three that bear record in heaven, the Father, the Word, and the Holy Ghost: and these three are one.
— 1 JOHN 5:7

In the beginning was the Word, and the Word was with God, and the Word was God.... And the Word was made flesh, and dwelt among us....
— JOHN 1:1,14

How can I make Jesus Lord of my life?

Jesus is the Living Word. And God has given us the written Word to unveil the Living Word to us.

Give the Word of God — primarily the New Testament — first place in your life. By doing so, you are putting Jesus first!

Let the Word of God govern your life. Let this Word be the Lord of your life. Let the Word dominate you. By doing so, you are really allowing Jesus to lord it over you — because Jesus and His Word are One.

We are living in an age when we need to get serious about spiritual matters, and we need to learn *what the Bible has to say* about love, life, home, marriage, and children.

Let the Word of God be your guide in life. When you do, you are making Jesus the Lord of your life. Then His written Word becomes the Lord of your life.

Confession: *Lord Jesus, You are the Lord of my life. I allow your Word to dominate me. I allow your Word to have dominion over me; therefore, YOU are lording it over me. You are dominating me. You are the Lord of my life!*

Lamp of the Lord

The spirit of man is the candle of the Lord, searching all the inward parts of the belly.
— PROVERBS 20:27

One translation of this verse reads, "The spirit of man is the *lamp* of the Lord. . . ." To put it into modern speech, you would say, "The spirit of man is the *light bulb* of the Lord. . . ."

What this Scripture means is that God will enlighten us — He will guide us — through our human spirits.

Christians, however, seem to seek guidance in every other way except the way God said it is going to come! They judge how God is leading by what their physical senses tell them; but nowhere does the Bible say that God will guide us through our physical bodies! They look at things from a mental standpoint; but nowhere in the Bible does God declare that He will guide us through our mentality, our intellect, or our minds!

God said that it is the spirit of man that is the candle of the Lord. So God *will* guide us through our spirits. God will guide you through *your* human spirit.

Confession: *I am a spirit. I have a soul. I live in a physical body. My spirit is the candle of the Lord. God my Father is enlightening me through my spirit. God is guiding me through my spirit.*

Led by the Spirit

For as many as are led by the Spirit of God, they are the
sons of God.   — ROMANS 8:14

The sons of God can expect to be led by the
Spirit of God.

Believers can expect to be led, or guided, by
the Holy Spirit. Jesus, referring to the time when
the Holy Spirit would come, said, "He will guide
you." So we don't have to look to man for guidance
— that's unscriptural. All of God's children have
the Spirit of God within and can expect to be
guided by Him.

In February 1959, Jesus appeared to me in an
open vision. I heard His footsteps coming into my
hospital room. He sat on a chair by my bed and
talked to me for an hour and a half about the
ministry of a prophet. One of the things He said
was, "The prophet's ministry is not set in the
Church to guide members and tell them what to
do. Under the Old Covenant, people would go to
the prophet to seek advice, or direction, or
guidance, because he had the Spirit of God and
they didn't. No one under the Old Covenant,
except the king, the priest, and the prophet, had
the Holy Spirit upon them. The people knew
nothing about the Spirit's leading. But under the
New Covenant it does not say, 'As many as are
led by the prophets, they are the sons of God.' It
says, 'As many as are led by the Spirit of God,
they are the sons of God.' "

Confession: *I am a child of God. I can expect to be led by*
the Spirit of God. He is leading me now.

Born of the Spirit

That which is born of the flesh is flesh; and that which is born of the Spirit is spirit. Marvel not that I said unto thee, Ye must be born again.
— JOHN 3:6,7

Under the New Covenant, every child of God has the Spirit of God. First, they are *born* of the Spirit. Then they can be *filled* with the Spirit. And they can expect to be *led* by the Spirit.

Born of the Spirit. The spirit of man is the part of man which is born again. The Christian's spirit has the life and nature of God in it. The inward man is born of God's Spirit and has the Spirit of God in him.

Filled with that Spirit. The born-again Christian can be *filled* with that same Spirit which he already has in him. And when he is filled with that Spirit, there will be an overflowing of that Spirit. He will speak with other tongues as the Holy Spirit gives him utterance (Acts 2:4).

Led by the Spirit. "For as many as are led by the Spirit of God, they are the sons of God." Even the born-again one who has not been filled with the Spirit, has the Spirit of God abiding in him — and he can expect to be led and guided by the Holy Spirit.

Confession: *I am a child of God. I am born of the Spirit of God. The Spirit of God leads me. He is leading me now. The Holy Spirit will rise up big in me. He will give illumination to my mind. He will give direction to my spirit. I am being led by the Spirit of God.*

A Well of Water

Jesus answered and said unto her, If thou knewest the gift of God, and who it is that saith to thee, Give me to drink; thou wouldest have asked of him, and he would have given thee living water. The woman saith unto him, Sir, thou hast nothing to draw with, and the well is deep: from whence then hast thou that living water? . . . Jesus answered and said unto her, Whosoever drinketh of this water shall thirst again: But whosoever drinketh of the water that I shall give him shall never thirst; but the water that I shall give him shall be in him a well of water springing up into everlasting life.

— JOHN 4:10,11,13,14

Bible scholars know that water is a type of the Holy Spirit.

Jesus Himself used water as a type of the Spirit. When Jesus told the woman at the well of Samaria that He was the Giver of living water, she got it confused with the water in the well — natural water.

Then Jesus said, "The water that I shall give . . . shall be . . . a well of water springing up into everlasting life."

He was talking about the New Birth, the well of living water within the believer.

Confession: *I have drunk the living water, and I thirst no more. I am born of the Spirit of God. God's Spirit is in me. A well of water is in me springing up into everlasting life.*

Rivers of Living Water

In the last day, that great day of the feast, Jesus stood and cried, saying, If any man thirst, let him come unto me, and drink. He that believeth on me, as the scripture hath said, out of his belly shall flow rivers of living water. (But this spake he of the Spirit, which they that believe on him should receive: for the Holy Ghost was not yet given; because that Jesus was not yet glorified.)
— JOHN 7:37-39

Jesus used water as a type of the Holy Spirit.

Notice that there are two different experiences referred to in our texts for yesterday and today. One, the New Birth, is a *well of water* in you, springing up into everlasting life. The other, the infilling of the Holy Spirit, is *rivers*. Not just one river — but rivers.

The water in the well (salvation) is for one purpose: It blesses you. It is for your benefit. But the rivers (the infilling of the Holy Spirit) flow out of you to bless someone else. The purpose of being filled with the Holy Spirit is so that you might be a blessing to others.

Some people say, "If you are born of the Spirit, you have the Spirit, and that's all there is to it." But, no, just because you've had one drink of water is no sign that you're full of water. There is an experience subsequent to the New Birth of being filled with the Holy Spirit — and as a result of being filled, rivers of living waters flow out of the belly (the spirit).

Confession: *I am filled with the Spirit of God. Rivers of living water flow from my innermost being.*

My Spirit Prayeth

For if I pray in an unknown tongue, my spirit prayeth, but my understanding is unfruitful.

— 1 CORINTHIANS 14:14

God is a Spirit. Man is a spirit. God contacts us and deals with us through our spirits. He leads us through our spirits. He does not communicate directly through our minds, because the Holy Spirit does not dwell in our minds. And God does not contact us through our bodies either.

It should be comparatively easy for Spirit-filled believers to locate the human spirit. Those tongues come from your spirit, down on the inside of you. You speak the words out physically — but they don't come out of the physical senses. You yield your tongue to your own spirit, and the Holy Spirit in your spirit gives you the utterance.

The tongues don't come out of your mind or your soul. When you pray in tongues, your mind, your understanding, is unfruitful. Your understanding doesn't know what you're saying.

When you pray in tongues, the words come out of your innermost being — your belly — your spirit. *All the leadings I've ever gotten, have come out of my spirit.* And most have come when I was praying in other tongues — when my spirit was active and in contact with God.

Confession: *When I pray in tongues, my spirit prays. My spirit is active and in contact with God. The Holy Spirit in my spirit gives me the utterance.*

Look Inside

What is it then? I will pray with the spirit, and I will pray with the understanding also: I will sing with the spirit, and I will sing with the understanding also.

— 1 CORINTHIANS 14:15

In every crisis of life, I've learned to look to my spirit inside of me. I've learned to pray in other tongues. And while I'm praying in other tongues, guidance comes up from inside of me, because *my spirit is active when I pray in tongues.* My mind is not active then; my spirit is active. And *it is through my spirit that God gives me guidance.*

Sometimes while I'm praying in tongues privately, I'll interpret what I've said; and through the interpretation, I'll get guidance. But this doesn't happen most of the time.

Most of the time, while I'm just praying in tongues, from somewhere way down deep inside, the knowledge of what God wants me to do will just rise up in me. (It's difficult to explain spiritual things in natural ways, but I can sense something rising up within me.) It begins to take shape and form, and although I can't always put it into words (because my understanding has nothing to do with it), I know exactly on the inside of me what direction I'm to take.

Confession: *I listen to my heart. I look to my spirit inside me. I am spirit conscious, because the Holy Spirit indwells my spirit. He gives direction to my spirit. He guides me through my spirit.*

Beareth Witness

The Spirit itself beareth witness with our spirit, that we are the children of God. — ROMANS 8:16

God is going to guide us. God is going to lead us. We have Scripture that says so: *"For as many as are led by the Spirit of God, they are the sons of God"* (Rom. 8:14).

How does God lead?

The sixteenth verse of Romans 8 gives us a clue: *"The Spirit itself* [Himself] *beareth witness with our spirit, that we are the children of God."*

You don't know you are a child of God because somebody prophesies that you are. You don't know you are a child of God because somebody says they feel like you are. That's not how you know these things. You are not a child of God because you had a vision. (You might, or you might not have a vision, but that's not what makes you a child of God.)

How, then, does the Bible say we *know* we are the children of God?

God's Spirit *"bears witness"* with our spirit. Sometimes you can't explain exactly *how* you know, but you just *know* it down on the inside of you. You have an *inward witness* that you are a child of God.

That's the number one way God leads His children — through the inward witness!

Confession: *I am born of the Spirit of God. God's Spirit bears witness with my spirit that I am a child of God. The Spirit of God leads me. He is leading me now.*

Number One: Inward Witness

He that believeth on the Son of God hath the witness in himself....

— 1 JOHN 5:10

The way God confirms the most important thing that can ever happen to you, is also the way God leads His children: by the inward witness.

The most important aspect of your life — becoming a child of God — is confirmed to you by God's Spirit bearing witness with your spirit, that you have been born again (Rom. 8:16). This will help you understand that the number one way God leads His children is through the inward witness.

That is almost always the way I am led. Yes, I've had revelations, and I've had God lead me in other ways, too. But most of the time, I am led by the inward witness.

And you can be too!

Confession: *I am a child of God. I have been born again. I am born of the Spirit of God. God's Spirit bears witness with my spirit that I am a child of God. As many as are led by the Spirit of God, they are the sons of God. I am a child of God; therefore, the Spirit of God leads me. He is leading me now. I trust Him, the Greater One. He will rise up big in me. He will give illumination to my mind. He will give direction to my spirit, for I am a child of God. I am being led by the Spirit of God. And the Spirit of God leads me, first of all, through that wonderful inward witness.*

Supernatural Guidance

... I will pray the Father, and he shall give you another Comforter, that he may abide with you for ever; Even the Spirit of truth; whom the world cannot receive, because it seeth him not, neither knoweth him: but ye know him; for he dwelleth with you, and shall be in you.

— JOHN 14:16,17

The inward witness is just as supernatural as guidance through visions, angels, and so on. It is not as *spectacular,* but it is just as *supernatural.*

Many people are looking for the spectacular, and they miss the supernatural that's right there all the time!

Let me go back to what Jesus said to me when He appeared to me in an open vision in February 1959 in El Paso, Texas. I heard footsteps coming down the hospital corridor, so I looked up to see who it was. When I saw Jesus standing in the doorway, it seemed like the hair on my neck and head stood straight up. Goose pimples popped out all over my body. Jesus was wearing a white robe and Roman sandals. He was about 5'11" tall and weighed about 180 pounds. He pulled up a chair and sat by my bed. During the hour and a half that He talked to me, He told me, "The number one way I lead all my children is through the inward witness."

Confession: *God's Holy Spirit is in me. He is in me to help me, to lead me, and to guide me. First, the Holy Spirit bears witness with my spirit that I am a child of God. Then He bears witness with my spirit in all other aspects of my life.*

Stop Light

Howbeit when he, the Spirit of truth, is come, he will guide you into all truth.... — JOHN 16:13

For the three days prior to my vision of the Lord, I had been trying to write a letter to a pastor, confirming a date I was to hold a meeting for him. I'd get half a page written to him and then I'd tear it up and throw it in the wastebasket. The second and third days I did the same thing.

As the Lord sat by my bedside, He said, "I'm going to show you how the inward witness works so you won't make the same mistakes you've made in the past. You see me now sitting here talking to you. This is the prophet's ministry in manifestation — and a manifestation of discerning of spirits [discerning of spirits is seeing into the spirit realm]. You hear me talking to you. And I am bringing you, through the vision, a word of knowledge and a word of wisdom. I'm telling you not to go to that church. The pastor wouldn't accept the way you minister. But I'm never again going to lead you this way. [And He hasn't.] From now on, I'm going to lead you by that inward witness you've had all the time. You had a check, a hesitancy, on the inside. And that is the way I'm going to lead you."

This inward check is like a stop sign. It's like a red light — way down on the inside.

Confession: *The Spirit of truth is come. He indwells me. He guides me. He is guiding me now.*

Green Light

*Thus saith the Lord, thy Redeemer, the Holy One of Israel;
I am the Lord thy God which teacheth thee to profit, which
leadeth thee by the way thou shouldest go.*

— ISAIAH 48:17

A pastor once asked me, "Brother Hagin, do you ever go to small churches?" I replied, "Yes, I'll go anywhere the Lord says to go." Then the pastor told me about his church and said, "If God ever speaks to you about it, we want you to come." But I just dismissed his invitation.

However, several months later when I was praying about something else, this conversation came back to me. Then every day it kept coming back. Finally, after about the fourth day, I said, "Lord, do You want me to go to that church?" And the more I'd pray about it, the better I'd feel on the inside of me about accepting that invitation. (This wasn't a physical feeling — but one I recognized in my spirit.)

Sitting by my bedside, Jesus referred to this. "The more you thought about it, the better you felt about it," He reminded me. "You had a *velvety-like* feeling in your spirit. That's the green light. That's the go-ahead signal. That's the witness of the Spirit to go. Now you see Me, and I'm telling you to go to that church. But I'm never going to lead you to go anywhere again like this. From now on, I'm going to lead you like I do every Christian — by the inward witness."

Confession: *The Lord leads me in the way I should go. He leads me by an inward witness.*

Abundant Provision

. . . let them say continually, Let the Lord be magnified,
which hath pleasure in the prosperity of his servant.
— PSALM 35:27

Here's something else the Lord said to me
during the vision I had in February 1959. It was
not just for my benefit, but for yours too.

He said, "If you will learn to follow that inward
witness in all areas of your life, I will make you
rich. I will guide you in all the affairs of life —
financial as well as spiritual. I'm not opposed to
my children being rich. I am opposed to their being
covetous." (Some people think the Lord is
interested only in their spiritual life — nothing else
— but He's interested in everything we're
interested in.)

The Lord has done for me exactly what He said
He would do — He has made me rich. Am I a
millionaire? No. That's not what the word "rich"
means. Rich means a full supply. It means an
abundant provision. I've got more than a full
supply. I've got more than an abundant provision.
It's because I learned to follow the leading of the
Holy Spirit — and this guidance came to me by
the inward witness.

God will make you rich, too, if you'll learn to
listen to the inward witness! Jesus said to me in
that vision, "Now you go teach my people how to
be led by my Spirit."

Confession: *The Spirit of God is leading me in all the affairs*
of life. He is leading me in spiritual matters. He is leading
me in financial matters. And I am listening to the inward
witness.

Light My Candle

For thou wilt light my candle: the Lord my God will enlighten my darkness. — PSALM 18:28

Sometimes even though the inward witness is there, people don't recognize it.

For example, I would be praying in tongues about the Sunday morning services in the church I was pastoring, and a burden for the church I had previously pastored, would rise up in me.

(Remember, when we pray in tongues, our spirit prays — and the spirit of man is the candle of the Lord.) That kept happening. After about thirty days, I said, "Lord, are You talking to me about going back there? If so, talk to my wife about it too."

One morning I said to Oretha, "Honey, if the Lord says anything to you, let me know." Then I waited another thirty days before I asked her, "Has the Lord been talking to you?"

She said, "If He has, I don't know it."

I got a little more specific about it. "Has the Lord said anything to you about going back to _____?"

"Oh," she said. "I thought that was just me."

Let's analyze that statement. When she said "me," if she meant the flesh, that wouldn't be right. But if she meant the real "me" — the man on the inside, which is the candle of the Lord — then it wasn't just her. *It was the Lord lighting the candle!*

Confession: *The Lord my God lights my candle. He enlightens me.*

47

On the Inside

*I will instruct thee and teach thee in the way which thou
shalt go: I will guide thee with mine eye. Be ye not as the
horse, or as the mule, which have no understanding: whose
mouth must be held in with bit and bridle....*

— PSALM 32:8,9

I knew by the inward witness that I should go
back to that church. And I knew my wife also had
the inward witness to go back. But I still wanted
the Lord to move in some "supernatural" way to
confirm it. (I was only 23 at the time.) I wanted
God to give me a word, tongues and interpretation, prophecy — or maybe even write up in the
sky, "GO TO THAT PLACE!"

So I fasted and prayed three days. The third
day I was on my knees, bawling, squalling, and
begging, because I didn't know any better, "Oooo
dear God ..."

And God said to me — for He leads by an
inward *voice* as well as by an inward *witness* —
"Get up from there and quit acting like that!"

I got up! But I said, "Lord, if You would just
give me a supernatural sign, I'd feel better about
going back to that church."

He replied, "You have all I'm going to give
you! You don't need any sign. You don't need any
writing in the sky. You don't need tongues and
interpretation, or prophecy. You know on the
inside what to do. *Now do it!*"

Confession: *The eyes of my understanding are being
enlightened. I know on the inside what to do. God leads
me by that wonderful inward witness. And I listen to it!*

Inside Signals

Who hath put wisdom in the inward parts? or who hath
given understanding to the heart? — JOB 38:36

God led us to move to Tulsa, by an inward
witness, in the late 1960s. Our home had been in
Garland, Texas, a suburb of Dallas, for seventeen
years. And we had no plans to move. In fact, since
our ministry was growing, I had it all planned just
how we would turn our entire house into an office
(we were operating the ministry out of our den and
garage) — and even how we could build additional
facilities on our property, if necessary.

Then we went to Tulsa on business. A friend,
in whose home we were staying, said to me,
"Brother Hagin, you need to move to Tulsa. And
I've got just the place for you! Brother T. L.
Osborn's old office building is for sale, and they've
asked me to sell it. Come on, I want to show it to
you." (Several people had tried to buy it, but the
deals always fell through, so the building was still
empty.)

I wasn't much interested, to tell the truth. But
I thought, *Just out of respect for my friend, I'll go.*

The minute I walked into that building, on the
inside of me, it was just like somebody had rung
a bell or set off a buzzer. Sometimes the inward
witness is like that. A buzzer went off in my spirit
— right down in my belly. It's difficult to describe,
but you just *know* it inside, in your spirit. This
was God confirming that He wanted this building
for my ministry.

Confession: *The Holy Spirit dwells in my spirit. Wisdom*
is in my inward parts. Understanding is in my heart. And
I listen to my heart.

Know-So Salvation

*No man hath seen God at any time. If we love one another,
God dwelleth in us, and his love is perfected in us. Hereby
know we that we dwell in him, and he in us, because he
hath given us of his Spirit.* — 1 JOHN 4:12,13

I was born again as a teenager on the bed of
sickness on April 22, 1933. Since that day, the
thought has never occurred to me that I might not
be saved.

Even as a young Christian, I would run into
people who would say, "You're not saved, because
you don't belong to our church." Or those who
would argue, "You're not saved, because you
haven't been baptized our way." And many others.

But none of it disturbed me. I laughed at it —
*because I had the inward witness: "The Spirit
itself beareth witness with our spirit, that we are
the children of God,"* Romans 8:16 says. And I had
the love: *"We know that we have passed from
death unto life, because we love . . . ,"* we read in
First John 3:14.

I had the witness — and I had the love. That's
why I never doubted my salvation. I walked in
love to the best of my ability — and I enjoyed the
witness of God's Spirit on the inside.

Confession: *I have the witness. The Spirit Himself bears
witness with my spirit that I am the child of God. I have
the love. I know that I have passed from death unto life.
God dwells in me. His love is perfected in me. I know I dwell
in Him, and He dwells in me, because He has given me of
His Spirit.*

Christian Equipment

But ye have an unction from the Holy One, and ye know all things.
— 1 JOHN 2:20

Even as a newborn babe in Christ, still bedfast, I would know things by an inward witness.

For example, my Mother said to me one day, "Son, I hate to bother you, but something is wrong with Dub." Dub, my older brother, had gone to the Rio Grande Valley to look for work. (He was 17 at the time.) Those were Depression days. Momma was a Christian, although not a Spirit-filled one, and she just had a witness of uneasiness and trouble in her spirit. "I don't know what it is," she said. "He may be in jail or something."

"Momma," I said, "I've known that for several days. But Dub's not in jail. His physical life was in danger, but I've already prayed, and he'll make it. Dub's all right. His life will be spared."

Three nights later, Dub came in. He hadn't found work, so he had decided to ride the freight trains home. A lot of people were "riding the rails" like that in those days. However, a railroad detective found Dub, knocked him in the head, and threw him off a train going 50-60 miles per hour. Dub slid on his back across the coal cinders that had fallen alongside the tracks. It's a wonder he didn't break his back — and he would have, if we hadn't known about it by an inward witness and prayed. We knew it because we were Christians.

Confession: *I have an unction from the Holy One, and I know all things.*

Learn To Listen

Howbeit when he, the Spirit of truth, is come ... he will shew you things to come. — JOHN 16:13

A minister friend of mine had three serious automobile accidents in less than ten years. People were killed in these accidents. His wife was almost killed, and the minister himself was seriously injured. Both he and his wife were healed by the hand of God. When he heard me teaching along these lines of listening to your spirit, the inward witness, he said, "Brother Hagin, every one of those accidents could have been avoided if I had listened to that inward intuition."

Yet people will argue, "I just don't know why those accidents happened to a good Christian. He's a preacher."

Well, he had to learn to listen to his spirit just like you have to learn to listen to yours.

People want to blame God and say that God did these things. But as this preacher told me, "If I had listened to the inward intuition I had that something was about to happen, I would have waited and prayed. Instead, I said, 'I'm busy. I don't have time to pray.' "

Many times, if we had waited on God when we had that inward witness, God would have shown us things, and we could have avoided problems. But let's not moan and groan about our past failures. Let's take advantage of our present opportunities, and make sure that we follow our inward witness in the future. Let's learn to develop our spirit — and learn to listen to it, and then obey it.

Confession: *I am becoming spirit conscious. I am developing my spirit. And I am listening to it!*

Where He Is

Jesus answered and said unto him, If a man love me, he will keep my words: and my Father will love him, and we will come unto him, and make our abode with him.

— JOHN 14:23

As Jesus goes on teaching in this fourteenth chapter of the Gospel of John, He begins to talk about the Holy Spirit coming to us: Jesus and the Father, in the Person of the Holy Spirit, come to abide in us.

At present, Jesus literally — with His flesh-and-bone body — is seated at the right hand of the Father. Yet the Bible talks about "Christ in you the hope of glory." You see, the reason why *Christ* is in us is because the *Holy Spirit* is in us.

The Holy Spirit said through Paul, "*Know ye not that ye are the temple of God, and that the Spirit of God dwelleth in you?*" (1 Cor. 3:16).

And in Second Corinthians 6:16 we read, "*. . . for ye are the temple of the living God; as God hath said, I will dwell in them, and walk in them; and I will be their God, and they shall be my people.*"

We've never plumbed the depths of what this is really saying: *God is dwelling in us!*

Therefore, if God is dwelling in us, then that is where God is going to speak to us — *where He is* — in our hearts, or our spirits. God communicates with us through our spirits. Our spirits pick things up from the Holy Spirit and then pass them on to our mind by an inward intuition, or inward witness.

Confession: *Make your confession from John 14:23, First Corinthians 3:16, and Second Corinthians 6:16.*

Number Two: The Inward Voice

I say the truth in Christ, I lie not, my conscience also bearing me witness in the Holy Ghost. — ROMANS 9:1

The number one way the Holy Spirit guides us is through the *inward witness.* The number two way is through the *inward voice.*

The inward man has a voice just as the outward man has a voice. We call the voice of the inward man "conscience." Sometimes it is also called intuition, inner guidance, inward witness, or "the still, small voice." It is *not* the voice of the Spirit of God speaking to us, because when the Holy Spirit speaks, His voice is more authoritative. The still, small voice is the voice of our own spirit. Yet our spirit picks it up from the Holy Spirit who lives inside us.

For example, I related in the devotion for July 19 how a "buzzer" seemed to go off inside me as I stepped inside that building that was for sale in Tulsa. I knew on the inside — *This is it!* But I didn't want to listen. When my wife asked about it later, I said, "No, we'll just stay where we are." But when we went to bed that night, I couldn't get to sleep. My conscience was hurting. My spirit knew I hadn't listened to it.

So I said, "Lord, in the natural, I don't want to move to Tulsa. But if that's what You want, I won't stand in your way." Suddenly, on the inside of me, that still, small voice said, "I'm going to give you that building. You watch Me." And God did just that!

Confession: *I listen to the voice of my spirit. And I obey it!*

Conscience

. . . while as the first tabernacle was yet standing: Which was a figure for the time then present, in which were offered both gifts and sacrifices, that could not make him that did the service perfect, as pertaining to the conscience. . . . How much more shall the blood of Christ, who through the eternal Spirit offered himself without spot to God, purge your conscience from dead works to serve the living God?

— HEBREWS 9:8,9,14

Is your conscience a safe guide?

Yes it is, *if* your spirit has become a new man in Christ. Remember Second Corinthians 5:17: *"Therefore if any man be in Christ, he is a new creature: old things are passed away; behold, all things are become new."* That's talking about the inward man, the spirit of man. Your conscience is the voice of your spirit speaking to you. If your spirit is a new man in Christ, with the life and nature of God in it, then it is a safe guide.

A person who has never been born again could not follow the voice of his spirit, or conscience, because his unregenerate spirit would have the nature of the devil in it. His conscience would permit him to do anything.

When you have the life and nature of God in you, your conscience will not permit you to do just anything. When you are a born-again Christian, the Spirit of God is living and abiding in your spirit!

Confession: *I am a new man in Christ, with the life and nature of God abiding in my spirit. Therefore, my conscience is a safe guide.*

Obeying Conscience

And Paul, earnestly beholding the council, said, Men and brethren, I have lived in all good conscience before God until this day.
— ACTS 23:1

It is interesting to go through the Epistles Paul wrote to the Church and see what he said about his conscience. He always obeyed his conscience.

Once I heard some preachers questioning one of the top evangelists in the world. They asked him, "We know God called and anointed you to stand in this ministry — but is there something that *you* do from the natural standpoint that contributes to the success of your ministry more than any other thing?"

I listened intently to hear what he would say. I knew he was a man of prayer, and prayer is important, but he didn't mention prayer.

He answered, "Of course, God called me to be an evangelist. But you are asking what has contributed to my success from *my* standpoint. And the one thing I do that has contributed to my success more than anything else is: *I always instantly obey my deepest premonitions.*"

In other words, what this evangelist was saying was, "I always obey what my spirit tells me — what I get right down on the inside of me."

Confession: *The Holy Spirit is in my spirit. He communicates with me through my spirit. My spirit has a voice. I obey what my spirit tells me — what I get down on the inside of me.*

When You Miss It

For if our heart condemn us, God is greater than our heart, and knoweth all things. Beloved, if our heart condemn us not, then have we confidence toward God.

— 1 JOHN 3:20,21

Does the Holy Spirit condemn you, if you, a Christian, do wrong?

No. It is *your spirit* that condemns you. This is something we need to learn. We haven't learned it yet, because we've been taught wrong.

The Holy Spirit will not condemn you. Why? Because God won't condemn you. Study what Paul wrote in Romans 8. He asked, "Who is it that condemns? Does God condemn? No, it is God who *justifies.*"

Jesus said that the only sin the Holy Spirit will convict the world of is the sin of rejecting Jesus (John 16:7-9).

I've found that even when I've missed it, the Holy Spirit in me is the One who shows me the way out. He comforts me. He helps me. He doesn't condemn me.

So it is your conscience, the voice of your spirit, that condemns you when you miss it.

It is your spirit that knows the very moment when you have done wrong.

Confession: *My spirit is born of God. My spirit is fed on God's Word. My spirit is indwelled by the Holy Spirit. Therefore, it is a safe guide. When my spirit warns me of wrong, I obey it instantly. For if my heart condemns me not, then I have confidence toward God.*

Inside Help

And herein do I exercise myself, to have always a conscience void of offence toward God, and toward men.

— ACTS 24:16

Soon after I was saved and healed, I returned to high school. Now, I don't know how it happened exactly — none of my family cursed — but we had a neighbor who could "cuss" up a storm, and I guess I picked it up from him. So at school one day, I said to one of the boys, "Hell, no . . ."

The minute I said it — and I didn't know a thing about the Spirit-filled life — in my heart I said, "O dear God, forgive me!"

What condemned me? The Holy Spirit? No. It was my own spirit. This new creature, this new creation, this new man, doesn't talk that way.

Now, the flesh may want to continue doing some things it used to do, or talking like it used to talk, but you have to "crucify" the flesh. And a good way to crucify the flesh is to bring any problems right out into the open immediately.

That's what I did when I realized I had cussed. I didn't wait until I was "moved" to repent; I immediately asked the Lord to forgive me. The young man I had said it to had walked away. I found him and asked him to forgive me. He said he hadn't even noticed what I'd said; he was used to people talking that way. But I wanted to get things right with him and with God.

Confession: *I am a new creature in Christ. I talk like a new creature. I think like a new creature. I act like a new creature. My spirit leads me to do so.*

Tender

Speaking lies in hypocrisy; having their conscience seared with a hot iron.
— 1 TIMOTHY 4:2

Keep a tender conscience — don't violate it — because it is your conscience, the voice of your spirit, that relates to your mind what the Spirit of God is saying to you down inside. If you don't keep a tender conscience, spiritual things will not be clear to you.

During the mid-'30s, I pastored a country church and usually spent Sunday nights in the home of a dear old gentleman who was about 89. He and I didn't get up as early as the rest of his family on this farm, so we had breakfast together about 8 o'clock.

He'd have one of those old-fashioned coffee pots sitting on the wood stove with the coffee just boiling in it. I've seen him pour that boiling coffee into a mug, hold it up to his mouth, and drink the whole cup of boiling coffee in one gulp. The first time I saw him do it, I felt like *I* was burning all the way down!

How could he do that? I certainly couldn't do it. My mouth and throat are so tender; one teaspoon of boiling coffee would have burned me. He couldn't do it either, to begin with. But through the years, drinking boiling coffee had seared this man's lips, mouth, and throat, until it was easy for him to drink that whole cup of boiling coffee in one gulp.

The same thing can happen spiritually. Keep a tender conscience. Stop the minute you miss it and your conscience condemns you. Say, "Lord, forgive me. I missed it." Or if you need to, tell someone you have wronged, "I did wrong. Please forgive me."

Confession: *I keep my conscience tender.*

The Dominant One

... Walk in the Spirit, and ye shall not fulfil the lust of the flesh.
— GALATIANS 5:16

I learned early in my Christian life to let my spirit, my inward man, dominate my outward man. So even as a teenage boy standing alone without the fellowship of other teenagers who believed like I did, I didn't have the problems some do.

If there was anybody in my Sunday School class who was saved besides me, I didn't know it. They would cuss, drink, attend worldly dances, and they were all mixed up with one another in sexual activities. They'd say to me, "Why don't you do these things?"

First, my conscience wouldn't allow me to do those things. Also, I'd reply to them, "I'm a new creature." And they would ask, "What's a new creature?" (That pretty well proved they weren't new creatures!)

You don't need to be preached to about do's and don'ts; just let your spirit dominate you. God will enlighten you through your spirit. Let the new man on the inside be the dominant one.

Don't let your body dominate you. Your body will want to keep on doing the things it's been doing, because your body hasn't been born again yet. Instead, walk by your spirit.

Confession: *I walk by my spirit. I let my spirit dominate me. I let the new man on the inside be the dominant one. Therefore I do not fulfill the lust of the flesh. I am not body ruled; I am spirit ruled.*

Spirit Walk

There is therefore now no condemnation to them which are in Christ Jesus, who walk not after the flesh, but after the Spirit.
— ROMANS 8:1

Conscience is the voice of the *human spirit.*
Reason is the voice of the *soul,* or the *mind.*
Feeling is the voice of the *body.*
The Holy Spirit does not bear witness with our reason. The Holy Spirit does not bear witness with our feelings. The Holy Spirit bears witness with our *spirits.*

I'm very careful about using the word "feeling." When we sense the presence of God in a service, people often say, "I felt it." But we really don't *feel it physically* so much as we *sense it spiritually.* So I am careful to differentiate between the two, because people slip into the feeling realm so easily. Then, when they feel good, they say, "Glory to God! Hallelujah! I'm saved! I'm filled with the Spirit! Everything is fine!" But when they feel bad, they get a long face and they say, "I've lost it all. I don't feel like I did, so I must be backslidden."

If we go by feelings, we'll get into trouble. That's why so many Christians are up and down, in and out. (I call them yo-yo Christians.) They don't walk by their spirits. They don't walk in faith. They go by their feelings.

Confession: *I walk not after the flesh, but after the spirit. I don't follow feelings. I don't follow reason. I follow the voice of my spirit, my conscience!*

Mountains and Valleys

Now thanks be unto God, which always causeth us to triumph in Christ.... — 2 CORINTHIANS 2:14

I hear people talk about being in the valley — and then on the mountain — and then back in the valley again. To tell the truth about it, I don't know what they're talking about. I've been saved since 1933, and I've never been anywhere but on the mountaintop!

You don't have to get down in the valley. People talk about their "valley experiences." I've never had any valley experiences. Oh, yes, there have been tests and trials — but I was on top of the mountain, shouting my way through it all, living above it. Praise God!

You see, those who say they're in the valleys are looking at life from the natural standpoint — from the physical. *They are trying to get a spiritual answer from the physical* — and you just can't do that.

Years ago, when I came among Pentecostal people after having been a Baptist, I'd hear them talk about "going through the valley." And when I didn't know what they were talking about, they'd look at me and say, "Your time's a-coming!" Thank God, it never has arrived!

No! Get off the negative and get on the positive side of life — and you won't have any valleys. You'll always be on the mountaintop!

Confession: *Thanks be to God, who ALWAYS causes me to triumph in Christ! I ALWAYS triumph! I live on the mountaintop!*

Stirred Up

Wherefore I put thee in remembrance that thou stir up the gift of God, which is in thee....

— 2 TIMOTHY 1:6

A woman got us out of bed at 2 o'clock one morning, crying, "If I could just get back to where I was with God!" I assumed she had committed some terrible sin, so I said, "Kneel down here and tell the Lord about it. He will forgive you."

She said, "I have searched my heart, and as far as I know, I haven't done anything wrong." I said, "Then what makes you think you have to get back to God?" "Well," she said, "I just don't *feel* like I used to."

I was visibly aggravated with her. I told her if I went by my feelings right then, she'd have to pray for *me!* But I showed her what to do: I told her to watch and listen as I prayed.

Then I said, "Dear Lord, I'm so glad I'm a child of God. I'm so glad I've been born again. I don't feel anything, but that doesn't have anything to do with it. My inward man is a new man. I want to thank You that I'm filled with the Holy Spirit. God the Father, God the Son, and God the Holy Spirit reside in me. I want to thank You for that ..."

I didn't feel anything, but I confessed it, because that's what the Word says. When I did, on the inside of me, something bubbled up.

"The expression on your face changed. Your face lit up," the woman said. "Yes," I said, "it was in me all the time. I just stirred up what is in me."

Confession: *I stir up what is in me!*

Faith — Not Sight

For we walk by faith, not by sight.

— 2 CORINTHIANS 5:7

Something Smith Wigglesworth said blessed me when I first read it way back in the late thirties, because it was so in line with my own experience. He said:

I am not moved by what I feel.

I am not moved by what I see.

I am moved only by what I believe.

Then he went on to say:

I can't understand God by feelings.

I can't understand the Lord Jesus Christ by feelings.

I understand God by what the Word says about Him.

I understand the Lord Jesus Christ by what the Word says about Him. He is everything the Word says He is.

You will not be able to understand yourself by feelings. Instead, understand yourself as a born-again, Spirit-filled Christian by what the Word of God says about you.

And when you read what the Word says about you — whether you feel like it or not — say, "Yes, that's me. I have that. The Word says I have that. I can do what the Word says I can do. I am what the Word says I am."

As you do this, you will begin to develop spiritually.

Confession: *I walk by faith and not by sight. (Now make Wigglesworth's confession, your confession.)*

Examine Your Leading

Knowing this first, that no prophecy of the scripture is of any private interpretation. For the prophecy came not in old time by the will of man: but holy men of God spake as they were moved by the Holy Ghost.

— 2 PETER 1:20,21

The Word and the Spirit agree.

How can you tell if it is the Spirit of God? If it is in line with the Word, then it is of the Spirit. If it is not in line with the Word, then it is not the Spirit.

I've had people tell me God was leading them to do something, and when I heard what it was, I said, "No, that's not the Spirit of God."

This is an extreme case, but it's true. A man told me he thought the Spirit of God was leading him and another woman to leave their spouses and marry one another. No! That is out of line with the Word! The Holy Spirit does not break up homes.

The Spirit and the Word agree! The Bible is inspired by the Spirit of God.

Examine your leading in the light of the Word.

Confession: *I am led by the Spirit of God. I examine my leading in the light of His Word, because the Word and the Spirit agree.*

Direction

Trust in the Lord with all thine heart; and lean not unto thine own understanding. In all thy ways acknowledge him, and he shall direct thy paths.

— PROVERBS 3:5,6

It is not for us to tell the Lord how to lead us. We are to let Him lead us any way He wants to!

But it is for us to find out from the Word of God how He does lead. And He leads, first of all, by the inward witness.

We can also see in the Book of Acts and elsewhere how at times some believers received guidance through a vision; others received guidance from an angel who appeared to them and told them certain things. Such phenomena, however, didn't happen every day in these people's lives. They occurred once or twice in the entire lifetime of some of them. So that's *not* the ordinary way God leads — but He can if He wants to.

Often God is trying to bear witness with our spirit — trying to guide us — but we won't listen, because we want something *spectacular,* such as a vision, or an angel. But we must remember that *anything God does is supernatural!*

Confession: *I trust in the Lord with all my heart. And I lean not to my own understanding. In all my ways I acknowledge Him, and He directs my paths.*

Fleeces?

A new heart also will I give you, and a new spirit will I put within you: and I will take away the stony heart out of your flesh, and I will give you an heart of flesh. And I will put my spirit within you....

— EZEKIEL 36:26,27

To receive guidance, some people put out what they call a "fleece" before the Lord. The New Testament, however, does not say, "As many as are led by fleeces, they are the sons of God."

"Yes," someone may say, "but Gideon put out a fleece back in the Old Testament."

Why go back under the Old Covenant? We've got something better under the New Covenant. The Old Covenant was for spiritually dead people. I'm not spiritually dead — I'm alive! I've got the Spirit of God in me!

Remember, Gideon was not a prophet, priest, or king. Only men who stood in those three offices, under the Old Covenant, were anointed by the Spirit of God. The Spirit of God was not personally present with the rest of the people. That is why every male had to present himself once a year at the Temple in Jerusalem.

The Shekinah glory — the presence of God — was kept shut up in the Holy of Holies. But when Jesus died on Calvary, the curtain that blocked the way into the Holy of Holies was ripped in two from top to bottom. God moved out — and He has never dwelled in an earth-made house since! He dwells in us!

Confession: *God's Spirit dwells in me! He is the Greater One, and He dwells in me!*

His Will

... that ye might be filled with the knowledge of his will
in all wisdom and spiritual understanding; That ye might
walk worthy of the Lord unto all pleasing, being fruitful
in every good work, and increasing in the knowledge of God.
— COLOSSIANS 1:9,10

It is dangerous for Spirit-filled Christians living
now, under the New Covenant, to put out fleeces.
This fleece business is in the realm where Satan
is god (2 Cor. 4:4).

"God, if You want me to do this, then have this
happen," people pray. That's a fleece. And Satan
can move in the sense realm. But God has a better
way of leading His children than by this hit-and-
miss method of fleeces!

It was only after I came over into Pentecostal
circles that I heard about fleeces. While I was
pastoring one church, the board of another church
asked me to try out to be their pastor. I preached
for them, and driving back home, I put out a fleece.

"Lord, I'm going to put out a fleece," I said.
"Here it is: If that church elects me 100 percent
— if I get all the votes — I'm going to accept it
as your will."

They elected me 100 percent. I moved there,
and I got fleeced! And they got fleeced. Both of
us missed God 100 percent! As I look back, I
realize that I had a check in my spirit all the time,
but I didn't listen.

Confession: *I pray that I might be filled with the knowledge*
of God's will in all wisdom and spiritual understanding;
that I might walk worthy of the Lord unto all pleasing,
fruitful in every good work; and increasing in the
knowledge of God.

Your Own Words

... He that sweareth to his own hurt, and changeth not.
— PSALM 15:4

Even though I missed God's perfect will by putting out a fleece, I stayed with that church one year, because I had promised them I would. I toughed it out. I'm a man of my word.

One of the characteristics of a spiritual pilgrim is that he "sweareth to his own hurt, and changeth not." In other words, he keeps his word.

If you don't learn to be a person of your word, your faith will never amount to anything. Why? Because to get faith to work for you, you have to believe in your *words* as well as believe in your heart: "*... whosoever shall SAY ... and shall not doubt in his heart, but shall believe that those things which he SAITH shall come to pass; he shall have whatsoever he SAITH*" (Mark 11:23). The things that you *say* are your words. And you're certainly not going to believe your word will come to pass when you know you're not a person of your word!

I'm going to keep my word. If I don't, it will affect my whole spiritual life. I tell the truth every time. I won't tell somebody I'm glad to see them if I'm not. I find some way to say something without violating my conscience. I won't lie, because it would affect my faith.

"But that's just being nice," someone will argue. No, it's not. It's being devilish.

Confession: *I am a person of my word!*

Waiting on God

But they that wait upon the Lord shall renew their strength; they shall mount up with wings as eagles; they shall run, and not be weary; and they shall walk, and not faint.

— ISAIAH 40:31

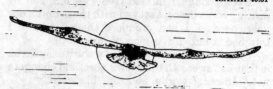

Except for that one time when I got fleeced, I never missed it when I made a change in churches or ministry.

"What did you go by — a fleece?"

No, I went by what the inward witness said. If I had to, I would wait a while before God. If I had to, I would wait all night long. If I had to, I might fast a day or so — not that fasting will change God. It won't.

God never changes. He's the same *before* I fast, *while* I fast, and *after* I fast. But fasting changes *me*. I would spend the time I would be eating in prayer and waiting on God. I would spend more time in the Word. Then my spirit man would become dominant.

So I waited until I knew on the inside of me what God wanted me to do. And I never got fleeced again.

Confession: *My spirit is the candle of the Lord. He guides me. He enlightens me. He leads me through my spirit. He leads, first of all, by the inward witness. He also leads by the still, small voice. He is leading. He is guiding. He is directing. I am Spirit led, Spirit taught, and Spirit guided.*

What My Heart Says

But thou shalt remember the Lord thy God: for it is he that giveth thee power to get wealth....

— DEUTERONOMY 8:18

I knew a man down in East Texas whose family was so poor that he didn't have a pair of shoes until he was 12 years old. He had only a fifth grade education. But way back when money was money, he had $2 million. He made his money in investments.

Two people who had been frequent guests in his home told me that he had said, "In many years of investing, I've never lost a dime."

Here's how he did it. He told my friend, "When someone comes with an idea and wants me to invest in something, my first reaction is mental. So I have a big closet I go into and pray about it. *I wait long enough to hear what my spirit says.*

"My head may say, 'You'd be a fool to invest in that,' but if my heart says, 'Go ahead,' I do. Or, my head may say, 'You'd better get in on this one,' while my heart tells me, 'Don't do it.' So I don't. *I don't pay any attention to my head.* I just get in that closet and wait — all night sometimes. And sometimes I'm in and out of it for three days, just praying and reading my Bible, getting quiet so I can hear what my heart says."

Confession: *The Holy Spirit guides me in all the affairs of life. And I listen to what my heart says!*

Prophets

But this shall be the covenant that I will make with the house of Israel; After those days, saith the Lord, I will put my law in their inward parts, and write it in their hearts; and will be their God, and they shall be my people.
— JEREMIAH 31:33

When Jesus appeared to me and told me to teach His people how to be led by the Spirit, He stated, "I didn't set prophets in the Church to guide people. The New Testament does not say, 'As many as are led by prophets, they are the sons of God.'

"New Testament believers," Jesus told me, "should not seek guidance through prophets. The prophets of the Old and the New Testaments are similar in some ways. Both see and know things supernaturally. But in the Old Testament, the people did not have the Spirit of God in them, or on them. They had a promise of the New Birth, but they didn't have it. So, if they were to be led by the Spirit, they had to go to somebody who was anointed with the Spirit. But under the New Covenant, every believer has the Spirit of God. They don't have to go to anybody to seek guidance. The only thing the prophet's ministry may do in this area under the New Covenant, is to confirm something somebody already has."

And if it doesn't confirm something you already have in your spirit, forget it!

Confession: *For as many as are led by the Spirit of God, they are the sons of God. God leads me!*

Born of God

Whosoever is born of God doth not commit sin; for his seed remaineth in him: and he cannot sin, because he is born of God. — 1 JOHN 3:9

People sometimes ask me, "How can I tell whether it is my own spirit or the Holy Spirit telling me to do something? It may just be me wanting to do it."

When you say "me," what are you talking about? If it is the real you — the man on the inside that's a new creature, with the life and nature of God in him, indwelt by the Holy Spirit — then it is right. If you mean "me," talking about the flesh, that's a different thing entirely. Learn to differentiate between the two.

A Christian's inward man isn't the one who wants to do wrong. If the inward man wants to do wrong, that person has never been born again.

First John 3:9 has bothered some Christians. They have made mistakes and failed, and they've thought, *If I were born of God, according to the Bible I wouldn't sin.* But this verse is talking about the inward man who doesn't sin.

I've done things that were wrong, but my inward man didn't do them. In fact, he didn't agree with me when I did them. He tried to get me not to do them. Physically, we are born of human parents, and we partake of their human nature. Spiritually, we are born of God, and we partake of His nature. And it is not God's nature to do wrong. Therefore, let your spirit dominate your flesh.

Confession: *I am born of God. My spirit has the life and nature of God, and its desires are right desires.*

Edification, Exhortation, Comfort

But he that prophesieth speaketh unto men to edification, and exhortation, and comfort.

— 1 CORINTHIANS 14:3

The following is a word of prophecy that came during a seminar I taught on being led by the Spirit:

Look inside, inside your spirit. For your spirit is the candle, the lamp of the Lord, searching all the inward parts of the belly. And so ye shall know, and ye shall walk in the light of that which ye know. No one will be able to gainsay thee, for thou wilt say, "There is light in my dwelling. I am the temple of the Holy Spirit. He dwells in me. He enlightens my spirit. Yea, I walk in that witness that's within my spirit. I do that which I know by an inward intuition. I follow that deep premonition in my innermost being. And so I am being led by the Spirit. I am rejoicing and I'm glad. Yea, I sound forth His praises evermore. I look to that which in me does reside. For residing in me is the potential of all that God has and is. All the attributes of even the Father God Himself reside within my spirit, and are potentially mine. For He has declared, "I'll walk in them. I'll live in them. I'll be their God. They will be my people." My God is not in a far-off distant land, out of reach and not at hand. My God sits not on a pedestal; nor can He be seen with the physical, or touched with the hand. My God is a Spirit who resides in man!

The Voice of the Holy Spirit

While Peter thought on the vision, the Spirit said unto him, Behold, three men seek thee. — ACTS 10:19

God leads by an inward witness. He leads by what we call the still, small voice — the voice of our own spirits. And he also leads by the Voice of the Spirit of God speaking to us. This is more authoritative than the still, small voice. When this Voice speaks, it is so real, you may look around to see who said it — even though it comes from inside you! There have been times I've heard the Voice of the Spirit and to me it was audible, although others near me didn't hear it. It must have seemed audible to the child Samuel, too, yet Eli the prophet didn't hear it.

This isn't the ordinary way God leads, however. I have found in more than fifty years of ministry that every time God has spoken in a spectacular way, such as in an audible voice (at least to me it was audible), there was rough sailing ahead. And if He hadn't spoken so spectacularly, I wouldn't have stayed steady.

The Bible tells us there are many voices in the world, and none of them without significance. This isn't a matter of listening to voices, however. Be careful about following anything without first examining it in the light of the Word. Don't pray to hear something. If God speaks to us, all right. If God doesn't speak to us, we have His Word, and we can walk in the light of it.

Confession: *I walk in the light of God's Word!*

Perception

Now when much time was spent, and when sailing was now dangerous, because the fast was now already past, Paul admonished them, And said unto them, Sirs, I perceive that this voyage will be with hurt and much damage, not only of the lading and ship, but also of our lives.

— ACTS 27:9,10

Paul didn't say, "I've got a revelation." He didn't say, "The Lord told me." He didn't say, "The Lord revealed it to me." He said, "I perceive. . . ." This was just an inward witness that he had. He perceived something spiritually.

A family of seven went out to eat. The children's food had already arrived at the table when the father suddenly said, "Let's rush home. I just have a perception that we should go." When they arrived, they found that a fire had started in their house. They were able to put it out. If we would become more spirit conscious, many things could be averted.

"Well, God did that. He had some purpose in it," people will say. No, we miss it because we don't listen. If the sailors had listened to Paul, they could have saved the ship and all the merchandise.

God is not an enemy of man; He is trying to help us. He is not working *against* us; He is working *for* us.

Confession: *The Spirit of the Lord is in me to help me. He is working for me. I perceive His direction and His help spiritually. I am spirit conscious.*

His Guiding Word

Thy word is a lamp unto my feet, and a light unto my path.
— PSALM 119:105

Don't seek guidance when the Bible has already told you what to do. Just go ahead and do it!

The Bible tells you how to act under every cirumtance in life.

It tells the husband how to treat his wife.

It tells the wife how to treat her husband.

It tells parents how to treat their children.

It tells children how to respond to their parents.

It tells all of us to walk in divine love. Divine love seeks not its own. It's not out for what "I" can get, but what "I" can give.

We have God's Word, and we can walk in the light of it. I go as much by what God *doesn't* say to me by the Spirit as by what He *does* say. If He doesn't say anthing, I just keep going in the direction I have been going. I just keep doing what I have been doing. I know God will tell me when to change. If He doesn't give me new directions, I don't worry about it. I don't "seek" anything. I just keep going.

Confession: *Your Word, O Lord, is a lamp unto my feet. It is a light unto my path.*

Guardian Angels

Take heed that ye despise not one of these little ones; for I say unto you, That in heaven their angels do always behold the face of my Father which is in heaven.

— MATTHEW 18:10

Years ago, a group of us were ministering to the Lord in prayer, such as is described in Acts 13:1,2. I had just gotten up off my knees and had sat down on the platform by a folding chair, still praying in other tongues, when suddenly Jesus stood right in front of me! And standing right behind Jesus, about two feet to Jesus' right and three feet behind Him was a large angel! The angel must have been 8 feet tall — a big fellow.

Jesus talked to me about some things (and everything He said later came to pass). When He finished what He was telling me, I asked Him, "Who is that fellow? What does he represent?"

Jesus answered, "That's your angel."

I said, "My angel?"

"Yes," He said. "You remember when I was on earth I said of little children that their angel is ever before my Father's face. *You don't lose your angel just because you grow up.*"

Isn't that comforting? Everywhere I go, I've got that big fellow following me around!

Confession: *According to Hebrews 1:14, angels are sent forth to minister FOR those who are the heirs of salvation. I am an heir of salvation. My angel is sent forth to minister for me.*

Guidance by Angels

Are they [angels] *not all ministering spirits, sent forth to minister for them who shall be heirs of salvation?*

— HEBREWS 1:14

Even as Jesus talked with me, I would glance at the angel. When I did, I could see he would start to say something.

Jesus said, "He's got a messsage for you."

I said to Jesus, "You're talking to me. Why don't You give me the message? Besides, the Word says, 'As many as are led by the Spirit of God, they are the sons of God.' I've got the Holy Ghost; why couldn't He talk to me?"

Jesus had mercy and was patient. He said, "Did you read in my Word where the angel of the Lord told Philip to go down the way unto Gaza? Wasn't that guidance? Didn't an angel give Cornelius directions?" Then He gave me several more New Testament illustrations of angels giving guidance.

Finally I said, "That's enough. I'll listen."

The angel started by saying, "I am sent from the presence of Almighty God to tell you . . . (and he spoke to me about a certain direction I was to take). You'll have $4000 in your hands by December 1 [this was 1963] to get you headed in this direction. For I've sent my angels out to cause the money to come."

On that date, I had exactly $4000 to the penny, just as he had said I would. That was the beginning of this ministry.

Confession: *I am an heir of salvation. My angel is sent forth to minister for me!*

Charged To Keep

For he shall give his angels charge over thee, to keep thee in all thy ways.
— PSALM 91:11

I heard a pioneer Pentecostal missionary tell this experience. A neighboring tribe kidnapped a little girl from the tribe where he was a missionary. The people in her tribe knew that if they didn't recover her before nightfall, they would never see her again.

So the missionary and a native interpreter made their way through the jungle to the kidnappers' village. They took trinkets and bargained with the chief for the child's return, but night overtook them. Because they couldn't travel at night in the jungle, they were forced to stay at the kidnappers' village. Sleeping on the floor of a thatched hut, they were awakened by the sound of drums. The interpreter said that the drums meant they were to be killed: The chief had decided to kill them and keep both the trinkets and the girl. Then they heard the hostile natives coming for them.

The missionary and the interpreter knelt down, prayed, and committed themselves to God. Then the missionary said, "Let's not wait for them. Let's go out. I'll go first."

He stepped outside with his eyes shut and waited for what seemed to be an eternity. One slash of their knives could cut off his head. But instead he heard moaning and groaning. He looked, and every native was on his face on the ground.

"They are calling you 'god,' " the interpreter said. "They say that when you stepped outside, two giants in white stepped out with you, holding great swords in either hand."

Confession: *God has given His angels charge over me to protect me in all my ways.*

Counsel Within

Counsel in the heart of man is like deep water; but a man of understanding will draw it out. — PROVERBS 20:5

Although God does lead through visions and other supernatural manifestations, I would encourage you *not* to seek a vision.

Do not seek visions or similar experiences. Why? Because you might get *beyond* the Word, where the devil can deceive you. (*See* Second Corinthians 11:14.)

Sometimes we would prefer to have a more direct word of guidance. But we don't always get it. So don't try to manufacture one if it doesn't happen. Nowhere does the Bible say that believers sought these experiences, or that they were seeking visions when they came. The visions just happened without people seeking for them.

Be content if all you ever have is the inward witness. Be content to follow that witness. But educate, train, and develop your human spirit to the point where that witness becomes more and more real to you.

Then, if God sees fit to give you supernatural visitations and manifestations, just thank Him for them.

Confession: *I will educate, train, and develop my human spirit so that the inward witness will become more and more real to me.*

Above Only

The Lord shall open unto thee his good treasure, the heaven to give the rain unto thy land in his season, and to bless all the work of thine hand: and thou shalt lend unto many nations, and thou shalt not borrow. And the Lord shall make thee the head, and not the tail; and thou shalt be above only, and thou shalt not be beneath....

— DEUTERONOMY 28:12,13

The reason why Christians continually make mistakes and fail is because their spirits, which should guide them, are kept locked away in prison, so to speak. Even in our churches, the intellect has taken the throne.

Any person who shuts his spirit away and never listens to it becomes crippled in life. He becomes an easy prey to selfish and designing people.

But the person who listens to his spirit is the one who climbs to the top.

Before I began to learn in 1959 how to follow the inward witness, it cost me financially. I had to borrow money to get out of a financial hole. Yet God had said I would have money to loan if I would follow Him. But I wasn't following God in this case. I hadn't yet learned to follow the inward witness. But when I began to follow it, I started rising to the top. And I've been rising ever since.

Confession: *Make your own confession from today's Scripture.*

Spirit Growth

That we henceforth be no more children, tossed to and fro, and carried about with every wind of doctrine, by the sleight of men, and cunning craftiness, whereby they lie in wait to deceive; But speaking the truth in love, may grow up into him in all things, which is the head, even Christ.

— EPHESIANS 4:14,15

If it is true that the spirit of man is the candle of the Lord, and if it is also true that God will enlighten and guide us through our spirits — and it is — then that part of us needs to grow. The spirit of man needs to be developed so it can be a safer guide.

Your spirit can be educated and trained, just as your mind can be educated.

And your spirit can be built up in strength, just as your body can be built up in strength.

I am well convinced that if you will follow the steps I will give over the next few days, you can train your spirit to the point where eventually you will always get an instant "yes" or "no" on the inside, even in the minor details of life.

You must realize this, though: You didn't start the first grade one day and graduate from high school the next day. It took time to develop your mentality. It also will take time to train, educate, and develop your spirit.

Confession: *I will take the time to train, educate, and develop my spirit. My spirit is growing!*

Meditating in the Word

This book of the law shall not depart out of thy mouth; but thou shalt meditate therein day and night, that thou mayest observe to do according to all that is written therein: for then thou shalt make thy way prosperous, and then thou shalt have good success. — JOSHUA 1:8

How can your spirit be educated and trained? How can your spirit be built up in strength? There are four steps: (1) Meditating in the Word; (2) Practicing the Word; (3) Giving the Word first place; and (4) Obeying your spirit. We will study these four steps in coming days.

What God said to Joshua will work for everybody. If God didn't want Joshua to be prosperous, why did God tell him how to prosper? If God didn't want Joshua to be successful, why did God tell him how to have good success? But God wanted Joshua to be prosperous and successful. And he wants *you* to be prosperous and successful too! Furthermore, God has given us directions in today's text.

Paraphrasing this truth into New Testament language, God simply said, "The Word of God [particularly the New Covenant, or New Testament] shall not depart out of your mouth. But meditate therein day and night . . . for then you shall make your way prosperous, and you shall have good success in life."

Confession: *The Word of God shall not depart out of my mouth. I shall meditate therein day and night. Therefore, I shall make my way prosperous, and I shall have good success in life!*

Day and Night

But his delight is in the law of the Lord; and in his law doth he meditate day and night. And he shall be like a tree planted by the rivers of water, that bringeth forth his fruit in his season; his leaf also shall not wither; and whatsoever he doeth shall prosper.
— PSALM 1:2,3

If you ever want to do anything great in life — if you ever want to amount to anything in life — take time to meditate in the Word of God. Start out with at least ten or fifteen minutes a day, and build up.

For many years, I held two services a day while in the traveling ministry. And in earlier years of field ministry, I would teach in the mornings, pray aloud all afternoon, and preach and minister at night. Because I ate only one meal a day during my meetings, I would grow weak expending all this physical energy.

Then the Lord spoke to me. He said, "Don't spend all that time praying and wearing yourself out for the night service. Lie on the bed and meditate." When I began to do that, my spiritual growth was greater than ever before.

Well, that's what God promised: "... *for then thou shalt make thy way prosperous, and then thou shalt have good success.*" I wanted to prosper and have good success in the ministry. But this works whether you are in the ministry, raise cows, or sell automobiles!

Confession: *I take time every day to meditate in God's Word!*

My Meditation

O how love I thy law! it is my meditation all the day.
— PSALM 119:97

A minister told me how he'd been trying to make a success of his church. If he heard of a pastor who was doing well, he would visit him and see what kind of program he had. Then he would try to put that man's program into action in his church — but it never worked. And he'd fly all over the country doing this.

Then the pastor decided he would meditate in the Word the way he'd heard me teach. So he took a little time out each morning to meditate on the Word. He told me that after thirty days of meditating on the Word, one Sunday they had a landslide response. More people were saved than in the previous two or three years; his people were revived — and he began to have good success.

The ministry was this pastor's life. That's where he needed to have good success. Your life calling may be different. But it is certainly true that your way can also be prosperous, and you can have good success. Take time to meditate in the Word. Shut yourself in alone with your spirit. Shut the world out.

Confession: *I will meditate in God's Word. I will observe to do what His Word teaches. My way shall be prosperous. I shall have good success in life. I shall know how to deal wisely in the affairs of life. For the Word of God says so.*

Practicing the Word

But be ye doers of the word, and not hearers only, deceiving your own selves. — JAMES 1:22

Your spirit can be developed by four things. We have just examined the first: meditation. Now we will look at the second: *practicing the Word.* Practicing the Word means being a doer of the Word.

There are *talkers* about the Word. And even *rejoicers* about the Word. But we don't have many *doers* of the Word.

Begin to practice being a doer of the Word. Under all circumstances, do what the Word of God tells you to do.

Some think that being a doer of the Word is simply keeping the Ten Commandments. No, that's not what James 1:22 means. After all, under the New Covenant, we have only one commandment — the commandment of love. If you love someone, you won't steal from him. You won't lie about him. Paul said that love is the fulfilling of the law. If you walk in love, you won't break any law that was given to curb sin. So, if you're a doer of the Word, you will walk in love.

But being a doer of the Word for New Covenant Christians means doing primarily what is written in the Epistles. Those are the letters written to the Church. They belong to us, and we are to do them.

Confession: *I am a doer of the Word, not just a hearer only!*

Refusing To Fret

Be careful for nothing; but in every thing by prayer and supplication with thanksgiving let your requests be made known unto God. — PHILIPPIANS 4:6

The *Amplified* translation of this verse begins, "Do not fret or have any anxiety about anything. . . ."

Christians usually practice only part of this verse — the part that says to pray. But if we practice that part and not the part about not having anxiety, we're not practicing the Word. We're not being a doer of the Word.

First, God's Word says, "Do not fret. . . ." If you're going to fret and be anxious, it won't do you any good to make requests. Your prayers will not work.

I read a story years ago about a man, his wife, and grown son who were all out in the field chopping cotton. The son wasn't quite right mentally. Storm clouds appeared, and it began to thunder, but the old man wanted to hoe out to the end. Then the lightning became bad. The family began to run for shelter. When it looked as though they weren't going to make it, the parents fell to their knees and began to pray. "Come on, Ma and Pa," the boy cried. "A scared prayer ain't no account."

There's much truth to that. That's what the Spirit of God is saying through Paul. So, when you pray, "Be careful for nothing. . . ."

Confession: *I do not fret or have any anxiety about anything.*

Doing Philippians 4:6

Do not fret or have any anxiety about anything, but in every circumstance and in everything by prayer and petition [definite requests] with thanksgiving continue to make your wants known to God. — PHILIPPIANS 4:6 *Amplified*

A minister once came to me for advice. There were many storms in his life, and I felt sorry for him. He couldn't eat or sleep.

Just to sympathize with him wasn't enough, so I had him read Philippians 4:6. "But everybody doesn't have the faith you have," he told me. "Yes, but they have the same Bible," I replied, "and it's a matter of practicing the Word."

Then I showed him how to practice the Word: I read a verse aloud and then told the Lord, "Your Word is true, and I believe it." When I first started practicing this verse, I believed I could make my requests known to God, but it was hard for me to believe I could keep from fretting. However, God won't ask us to do something we can't do. So when God said not to fret, this means we can keep from fretting.

So I say aloud, "I refuse to fret or have any anxiety about anything." Then I bring my requests to the Lord and thank Him for them. This quiets the troubled spirit the devil tries to make me have. If the devil tries to get me to worry again, I simply go back, reread this verse, and keep claiming it.

Confession: *I am a doer of Philippians 4:6!*

Doing Philippians 4:7,8

*And the peace of God, which passeth all understanding,
shall keep your hearts and minds through Christ Jesus.
Finally, brethren, whatsoever things are true, whatsoever
things are honest, whatsoever things are just, whatsoever
things are pure, whatsoever things are lovely, whatsoever
things are of good report; if there be any virtue, and if there
be any praise, think on these things.*

— PHILIPPIANS 4:7,8

Many people want what verse seven talks
about, but they don't want to do what verse six
says to do in order to get it. In order to get what
verse seven says, you have to practice the sixth
verse, which we studied yesterday.

People who worry and fret, continually think
on the wrong side of life. They continually talk
unbelief. If something isn't true, honest, just, pure,
lovely, and of a good report, then don't think about
it. Make it meet all these qualifications. Some
things you hear may be true, but they may not be
pure and lovely — so don't think about them. To
do so is to give place to the devil, who is always
seeking to enter your thought life. That's why the
Bible says, "Think on these things."

Meditate and feed on the letters written to the
Church. Through them, God speaks to his Church.

Confession: *I do not fret or have any anxiety about
anything. Therefore, the peace of God keeps my heart and
mind through Christ Jesus. I think on those things that are
true, honest, just, pure, lovely, and of a good report!*

Giving the Word First Place

Thy testimonies also are my delight and my counsellors.
— PSALM 119:24

When the crises come — when the tests come — too many Christians say, "What are we going to do now?"

The crises of life come to us all. But if you are Word oriented, the first thing you will think about is, "What does *the Word* say about it?"

I pastored nearly twelve years, and I found that churches have problems just like families do. They have discipline problems, financial problems, and so forth.

I never discussed church problems with the people, because the more you talk about problems, the bigger they seem to get. But sometimes my deacon board would talk about church problems, and, sure enough, the more they talked about them, the bigger the problems seemed to get. Then one of them would look at me and say, "Oh, Brother Hagin, what in the world are we going to do?"

I'd smile and say, *"We're just going to act like the Bible is true!"*

Making that little statement would cause those deacons to sigh with relief. "It *is* true, isn't it?" they'd say. "Sure it is," I'd say.

It's amazing how things would straighten out when we acted like the Bible is true!

Confession: *Lord, thy testimonies are my counselors. I put them first. I put God's Word first. I act like it's so.*

Obeying Your Spirit

All scripture is given by inspiration of God, and is profitable for doctrine, for reproof, for correction, for instruction in righteousness: That the man of God may be perfect, throughly furnished unto all good works.

— 2 TIMOTHY 3:16,17

Did you notice that meditating in the Word, practicing the Word, and giving the Word first place — the first three steps in training the human spirit — come *before* obeying your spirit?

If your spirit has had the privilege of meditating in the Word, of practicing the Word, of putting the Word first, then your spirit is an authoritative guide.

In the process of time, if you will follow the four steps we have just studied, you can know the will of God even in all the minor details of your life!

But for this to happen, God's Word, not human reasoning, must dominate your thinking. The Word has been given to us by the Holy Spirit. *If the Word is dominating us, then the Holy Spirit is dominating our thinking!*

The written Word was given to us to develop, shape, form, and fit our spirit nature — and *nothing* but the Word will accomplish this. Reading about the Word won't do it. That's the reason why God wants us to meditate in His Word.

Confession: *God's Word is good. I meditate in God's Word. I observe to do what His Word teaches. My way shall be prosperous. I shall have good success in life!*